HANDCRAFTED INDIAN
ENAMEL JEWELLERY

ISBN: 81-7436-247-9
© **Roli & Janssen BV 2004**
Second impression 2006
Published in India by Roli Books
in arrangement with Roli & Janssen BV
M-75 Greater Kailash II (Market), New Delhi 110 048, India
Ph: ++91-11-29212782, 29210886 Fax: ++91-11-29217185

E-mail: roli@vsnl.com Website: rolibooks.com
Editors: Sujata Pandey, Dipa Chaudhuri. *Design:* Arati Subramanyam

Layout: Naresh Mondal, Kumar Raman. *Production:* Naresh Nigam
Printed and bound in Singapore

*Previous page: Once worn by a Vaishnavite devotee, this enamelled pendant
displays the feet of Lord Vishnu. (National Museum, New Delhi.)*
*Facing page and above: This handsome turban jewel set with a ruby, diamonds
and emeralds, is hung with Basra pearls. A beautiful example of Mughal jewellery,
it is as stunning on the reverse side, which displays the art of Indian enamelling
at its best. (National Museum, New Delhi.)*

HANDCRAFTED INDIAN ENAMEL JEWELLERY

RITA DEVI SHARMA • M. VARADARAJAN

India Crest

Lustre Press
•
Roli Books

ACKNOWLEDGEMENTS

We gratefully acknowledge the help and co-operation of the authorities at the National Museum, New Delhi, and the Victoria & Albert Museum, London for providing the photographs and granting permission to publish them in this book. We are thankful to Shri Jayant Chowlera, Ms. Anamika Pathak, Shri K.K. Sharma, Dr. R.K. Tewari and all the craftspeople working in this field who were generous with their time and discussed various aspects of enamelling with us.. We are equally thankful to Shri J.C. Arora, Shri Tejbir Singh and their colleagues for photographing some of the objects that figure in this book, and to Ms. Shefali Rathi, Ms. Chhavi and Ms. Sangeeta for helping us type the manuscript.

~

Below: This enamelled medal, inspired by the French Legion d'Honneur and set with emeralds and rock crystal, is from the collection of Dalip Singh, son of Maharaja Ranjit Singh of Punjab. This piece was crafted in Lahore. (Victoria & Albert Museum, London.)
Facing page: A kundan *and enamelled bracelet with* makara *heads. (National Museum, New Delhi.)*

CONTENTS

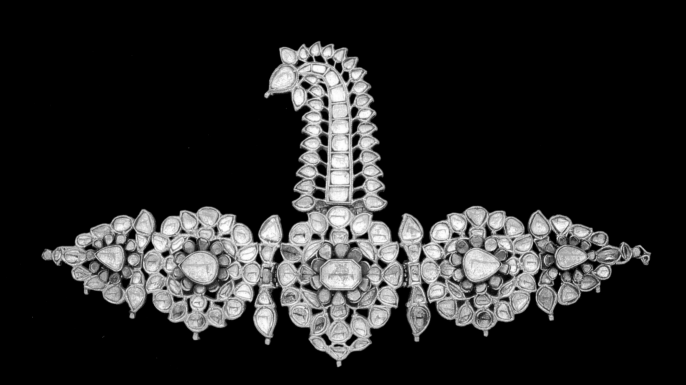

INTRODUCTION

*The reverse side of the same piece shows exquisite enamelling in red and green
with a floral design. The* sarpech *(turban ornament), is from the
late Mughal period. (National Museum, New Delhi.)*
Facing page: *A* sarpech *in gold and silver studded with
diamonds from the nineteenth century.*

~

These pendants display various styles and themes preferred by the Indian enamellers of the nineteenth century. The two on top show the idol of Shrinathji, while the central one has his name inscribed on it. The lower two bring out the brilliant green and blue plumage of the peacock. (National Museum, New Delhi.)

Indian jewellery is known the world over for its diversity of range and craftsmanship. Of all the different forms of jewellery that are crafted in India, enamelling is perhaps one of the most outstanding styles in brilliance and expertise. However, as there is no accurate, verifiable history of enamelling in India or in the surrounding regions, the exact date of its origin in the subcontinent becomes difficult to pinpoint. When did this fascinating craft start in India? This question is worth debating because it is generally accepted that the technique of enamelling is not an indigenous Indian craft but had its origins abroad.

In his book, *Industrial Art Of India,* Sir George Birdwood observes: 'It is probably a Turanian art. It was introduced into China, according to the Chinese, by Yüeh-chih, and was carried as early as, if not, earlier into India. From Assyria it probably passed into Egypt, and through the Phoenicians to Europe. Sidon was as famed for its glass, as was the Tyre renowned for its purple; and the Sidonians were not only acquainted with glass blowing, but also with the art of enamelling in glass in imitation of the precious stones.'

Sir George Birdwood also comments on the quality and the brilliance of Indian enamellings: 'It is the mingled brilliances of its greens, and blues, and reds which, laid on pure gold, make the superlative excellence and beauty of Jaipur enamelling. Even Paris cannot paint gold with the ruby, coral red, emerald green and turquoise and sapphire blues of the enamels of Jaipur, Lahore, Benares and Lucknow.'

He goes on to say: '...the art is practised everywhere in India, at Lucknow, Benares, at Multan and Lahore, and in Kangra and Cashmere, but nowhere in such perfection as at Jaipur.'

The earliest samples of enamel using glass can be traced back to before 2500 BC to the Sumerian and Egyptian civilizations. The craftsmen of those times inlaid coloured pieces of glass in small cells that were shaped by turning the edges of the thin gold sheets upwards. These upward turned metal edges also imparted the form to the ornament. Another method they employed was using little strips of gold sheet set on the edge of the front plate and soldered onto the back plate. Perhaps it did not occur to the craftsman that these compartments could be filled with coloured glass and fused *in situ*.

It was a goldsmith from Cyprus who, around the third century BC, initiated the technique of enamelling by fusing glass on to the metal substance. The earliest examples of this technique are six enamelled gold rings, which were discovered in 1952 in a Mycenaean tomb at Konkila in Cyprus. This discovery was a milestone in understanding the evolution of this fascinating craft.

Enamel jewellery was first introduced to Greece in the fifth century BC, and an example is a hair ornament of this period made of gold and silver, now in the collection of the Birmingham Museum. This is decorated in the shape of shields in gold cloisonné around an enamelled lion's neck. Another example is a golden sceptre of the fourth century BC, from Tarentum, now housed in the British Museum, London. The sceptre is in the shape of a cylindrical shaft covered with fine filigree work. On each intersection of the gold wires is a small dot of blue enamel. However, the use of enamel in Greek jewellery is minimal as there have been no findings of any large enamelled object from Greece till date.

In the first century BC, when the Romans subdued the Celtic tribes

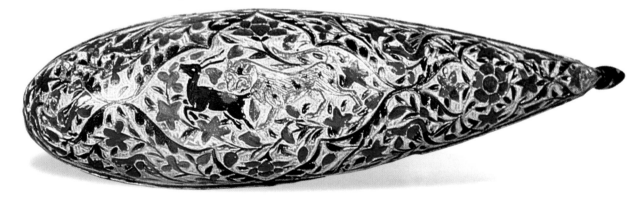

of Britain, they found equestrian trappings of bronze, armour and jewellery used by the Celts decorated with enamel. Some examples of these items sport spots of red enamel fixed in the recesses cut into the cast bronzes of the bridle bit or a mirror. A beautiful example of such work is from Birdlip, currently in the Gloucester Museum. The most striking examples of beautiful champlevé enamel of later eras are the hanging bowls found in the grave of a presumably Anglo-Saxon king from the Sutton Hoo Ship Burial, dated to the seventh century, in Suffolk, England, now in the collection of the British Museum.

There is no mention of enamelling in early Indian texts before the fifteenth century. The only available reference found on this subject is in the *Ain-i-Akbari* written in the sixteenth century by Abu'l Fazl, during the reign of the Mughal Emperor Akbar. According to Fazl, '...the *meenakar* or enameller works on cups, flagons, rings and other articles with gold and silver. He polishes his delicate enamels of various colours, sets them in their suitable place and puts them to fire. This is done several times over.'

Manuel Keen, author of *The Treasury of the World,* notes that, 'Despite the lack of a pre-existing tradition of enamelling in India, the art had already become established in the Imperial workshop during Akbar's reign.' This suggests that not only was enamelling practised during the reign of Emperor Akbar but that it was a well-established art all over the Mughal Empire as the technique of enamelling is believed to have spread to other parts of the country from the imperial Mughal *karkhanas*.

The jewellery produced in the imperial *karkhanas* combined Mughal finesse with a love for the sumptuous *meenakari*, or enamelling, a unique combination of gems, enamel pigments and precious metals. This became a quintessential symbol of the Mughal version of 'paradise on earth'. Confirming to Islamic precepts, this paradise was a celestial garden with all manner of trees, a riot of flowers and colours of every imaginable hue. The motif

consisted primarily of flowers, plants, scrolling vines and animal forms. Though an established craft, enamelling had not come into its own in the early Mughal period. It was Shah Jahan's aesthetic version that transformed enamelling into a sophisticated art form, which embellished a range of items from precious jewellery to imperial thrones. Borrowing ideas from his two major passions, architecture and fine gems, Shah Jahan took motifs from one and colours from the other, to inspire an art form, which henceforth was completely identified with Mughal aesthetics. *(Dance of the Peacock: Jewellery Traditions of India.)*

Different styles and fashions travelled with their owners along with craftsmen from their regions as people relocated either for monetary reasons or because of marriage alliances. The Mughal court saw the advantages of strengthening and expanding the boundaries of the Mughal Empire through alliances of marriage with Hindu princesses and with the granting of high positions to the Hindu nobility.

'During the eighteenth century, the artistic productions of most of the Empire had their foundations entirely in Mughal aesthetics. Some areas, such as Rajasthan, were able to resist being completely overwhelmed, though it is difficult to isolate specifically Rajput forms or motifs on unprovenanced jewellery. This is because Rajasthan undoubtedly contributed a great deal to the formation of the hybrid Mughal style: its princesses married to Mughal royalty and its rulers had taken high positions at Court, both bringing their jewellery and, probably, their craftsmen with them.' (Stronge, Smith and Harle.)

Early characteristics of enamelling containing Greco-Roman influences were also known in India. This can be observed from the various beads found in excavated Buddhist sites at Taxila in Pakistan. There are two types of beads: white enamel on a black cornelian

background, and a black enamelled pattern on a greyish white agate base. The enamelled designs are mainly pentagonal and hexagonal circles with dots in the centre or fine rows of little spots or two to three strips around the beads to form the symbol of the trinity. This type of enamelling has an almost distant relationship with the Indian enamelling of the Mughal period.

Certain experts have traced the origin of enamelling to the thirteenth century on the basis of a similar technique of manufacturing ornamental glazed tiles, which incidentally were also an important feature of Sultanate architecture. It is thus possible that the roots of Indian enamelling go back to that era.

Meanwhile in Europe, the art of enamelling had become a highly developed skill. Thus it was natural for Indian craftsmen to turn to European master craftsmen to learn their art and technique. So well did they learn the art that, in due course, they outshone their teachers. The many varieties of enamels of the Mughal period were based directly on the highly developed schools of enamelling in the West. The diverse unbroken lines of the different ranges of enamels can be used as a window to trace the evolution of the

Birds are beautifully depicted in each pendant against the white background at the back of this Nav-ratna *necklace. (National Museum, New Delhi.)*

The clasp of a Mughal bracelet (front and back) with beautiful floral and bird motifs, is executed using the champlevé technique. (National Museum, New Delhi.)

technique of enamelling through the centuries. Numerous existing specimens of Mughal jewellery point to this, with the forms being Indian and the designs and colour schemes being purely European.

In one miniature painting of Murshidabad now in the collection of Victoria & Albert Museum, London, Nawab Aliverdi Khan is shown holding the turban jewel of his grandson and designated successor, Siraj-ud-Daula. The jewel is almost identical to the one given to Admiral Watson in 1757 by Mir Ja'far, the Nawab who ousted Siraj-ud-Daula with the help of the British. This shows that provincial rulers took over stock imperial imagery in the way they were depicted in the painting.

With each successive political change and wars waged by foreign invaders in India, many of the famed pieces of jewellery and enamels found their way to different countries; some were taken as far away as to Tsarist Russia and England.

In 1739 AD, an Iranian ruler, Nadir Shah, sacked and looted Delhi. Much of what was taken by him became a part of the Crown Jewels of Iran. Other pieces—jewels and gold vessels studded with precious stones, or enamelled—were gifted to Russia by Nadir Shah in 1741 and are now in the Hermitage. *(The Golden Treasury.)*

Since royalty had an all-consuming interest in jewellery and its related arts, they employed many jewellers and associated craftsmen in royal ateliers. There are also accounts of artists' delegations and other contacts between the Mughal court and the Portuguese enclave of Goa during the reign of Akbar, in the seventies of the sixteenth century.

Although the arts and crafts in India were always treasured, they reached their zenith during the rule of Emperor Shah Jahan who was not just a prolific builder but who also had a keen eye for gems and jewellery.

The *Shah Nama* (a record of the life and times of Emperor Shah Jahan) makes repeated reference to enamelled objects. These objects were highly prized, and were clearly intended for the privileged few. Particularly pleased by a display of valour by his son, Aurangzeb, imperial largesse to the young prince on his fifteenth birthday according to the *Shah Nama* included

The jewellers of the Mughal court married the sophisticated designs and techniques of the Persians with Indian motifs and colours to produce some of the finest examples of enamelling anywhere in the world. These beautiful enamelled boxes are now in the National Museum, New Delhi.

~

A poetic composition in red and green with touches of white, this is the reverse side of a turban ornament, embellished with the famous Jaipur meenakari *work. An eighteenth-century piece, now in the Victoria & Albert Museum, London, it shows the influence of Mughal designs and craft traditions on Rajasthani enamellers of medieval times.*

~

two Qibchaq horses, one with a jewelled saddle, and the other with an enamelled one. Swords and shields with enamelled appurtenances were also singular marks of honour.

The imperial annals also record the emperor's first ascension on an enamelled throne constructed in the course of nine months for the sum of five lakh rupees.

One single instance confirms the excellence of and demand for the art of enamelling in Shah Jahan's time. This is the royal librarian's record of a golden screen. This magnificent object with enamelled inscriptions and cupolas was specially crafted to place around the tomb of Mumtaz Mahal, Shah Jahan's beloved queen, on her second death anniversary. *(Dance of the Peacock: Jewellery Traditions of India.)*

There is also one group of art historians which holds that the Mughal Emperor Humayun brought with him enamellers from Iran after his exile there in the sixteenth century. While this appears incorrect as Iran had no tradition of enamelling until the eighteenth century, nevertheless there are important substantiations in the accounts of seasoned and observant travellers like Jean-Baptiste Tavernier and Sir John Chardin. These observations seem authentic, as they were made by experienced travellers with a keen eye. Such 'experts' were not only intimately acquainted with the higher echelons of society, they were also knowledgeable professionals in the field of jewellery trade.

It is also quite probable that the art of enamelling was patronized at certain centres in the Deccan (in the south of India) even before the Mughals. From the sixteenth century onwards the art of enamelling spread from Mughal ateliers to other parts of the country.

'Technically, jewellery of the South differs greatly from that of the Mughal-influenced areas of India. The precious metal acts both as support and decoration, enamel is not usually found and gemstones tend to be used for their symbolic value rather than primarily for their decorative effect'. *(A Golden Treasury.)*

The jewelled hilt of a dagger from Rajasthan, has a ram's head studded with precious stones. (National Museum, New Delhi.)

TYPES OF ENAMELLING

Facing page *and **above:** This gem-studded early nineteenth-century enamelled gold head ornament (jhumar) hung with enamelled fish dangling from pearls, has a dancing peacock crafted in enamel. (National Museum, New Delhi.)*

~

A Hansuli *(necklace)* studded with precious stones and skirted with pearls. The underside *(seen above)* is enamelled in red, green, white and mauve. This stunning piece of Mughal craftsmanship is now in the collection of the National Museum, New Delhi.

20

Although the exquisite craft of creating jewellery flourished in all parts of the Indian subcontinent during the medieval period, the most beautiful pieces were produced during the Mughal era. The style during that period was to decorate the frontal side of the ornaments on an enamelled background with precious gems while the reverse was adorned with enamelled patterns. It is interesting to note that frequently the exquisitely enamelled backs of the pieces outshone the beauty of the gem-studded frontals of the ornaments.

The Mughal rulers of India had such a fondness for art and jewellery that they commissioned artists and jewellers from all over the empire and from abroad to make some of the most exquisite items for their personal adornment. The jewellers of the Mughal court married the sophisticated designs and techniques of the Persians with Indian motifs to produce some of the finest pieces of enamelled jewellery ever produced.

This effortless blending of Muslim and Hindu decorative art in the realm of jewellery made these pieces stylistically unique. At the same time, while the merging of the two cultures produced a stunning and grand display that left the viewers of these magnificent pieces bedazzled, it is also a perfect reflection of the rich composite culture of the subcontinent under the Mughals. Sadly, very few pieces of old gold and silver jewellery have survived since old jewellery was often melted down and the metal reused to make new ornaments to keep up with changing tastes and fashions. Luckily, enamelled pieces were largely preserved in their original form, because their beauty and value was dependent on the enamel work, which would be lost if they were melted down.

Some Rajput rulers (Suryavanshi) *traced their ancestry to the Sun. This gem-studded early nineteenth-century necklace from Udaipur, Rajasthan, (National Museum, New Delhi) with the Sun motif was probably commissioned by a royal patron.*

The reverse side of the same necklace, with Jaipur enamel work, has dainty floral motifs in green and red on a startling white background.

Certain regional variations, particularly in the schools of enamelling, have developed and can be seen by comparing the jewellery shown in the painting of that period with the Gentil album of 1774 (Stronge, Smith and Harle).

Enamels may be divided into five groups according to the treatment of the enamelled objects:

1. Enamelling done only on a single side or only on the frontal side of the object is known as *agari ko mina* (enamel on the front) or *ek posta* (single sided) in Rajasthan.

   Sometimes the enamelling is done only around the stone setting; this is generally in a green or blue colour and in a few cases the colour red is used.

2. Enamelling done on the back of an object is known as *pichhari ko mina* (enamel on the back) or *pharfura mina* (enamelling done on the reverse of a round object). The frontal side of the ornament in this kind of item is often gem-studded.

3. Enamelling done on both sides of a hollow jewellery piece, where one side has one or more openings (grooves) for gem settings is known as *do posta* (two sided). The frontal side of this kind of item is normally slightly convex, with square sides and a flat back.

4. Enamelling done on the straight sides of three-dimensional, hollow objects is known as *pahulpur ko mina* (three-dimensional enamelling).

5. Three-dimensional enamelling is known as *sub jagah ko mina* (enamelling all over). This type of enamelling is generally seen on round objects, such as decorative forms of birds, chess pieces and the like.

The background colours for enamels on the front of a gem-studded piece are usually selected to contrast with the colours of the gems. Diamonds or colourless stones are usually set on a *nili, sabz* or *lal zamin* (blue, green or red background), while emeralds are set on blue fields, but very rarely on a red or white field.

The colours and the combinations used on the back of the objects are design based. Generally, birds are illustrated in white, blue, green or turquoise, flowers in combination colours of red and white, red and yellow, pink and blue while the foliage

This necklace with enamelled pendants from Jaipur, has different colours on the front and back. (Victoria & Albert Museum, London.)

is in green. Geometric patterns are usually depicted in any of the many colour combinations.

Jaipur, Delhi, Benares, Deccan, Lucknow, Rampur, Kashmir, Kutch, Multan, Bahwalpur, Sindh, Himachal Pradesh, Punjab and Delhi were the regions where the best forms of enamelling were produced.

JAIPUR

The most reputed of all the centres of enamelling in India is Jaipur. The enamellers of Jaipur have reached such perfection in this craft that they remain unsurpassed throughout the length and breadth of the country. Jaipur—and to some extent Alwar—had the distinction of being the best-known centres for enamelling during the eighteenth and nineteenth century.

Jaipur was the enamelling centre 'par excellence' in the eighteenth and nineteenth centuries, the craftsmen traditionally being thought to have come from Lahore. (*The Golden Treasury*)

Rustam J. Mehta says in *Handicrafts and Industrial Art of India*: 'Jaipur is most famous for its beautiful enamelled jewellery. Here at Jaipur, the colours employed rival the tints of the rainbow in purity and brilliance, and they are laid on gold with such exquisite taste that there is never a want of harmony.' No wonder it is said that craftsmen of Jaipur 'could enamel rainbow tints on gold'.

Enamelling was initiated in Jaipur during the reign of Sawai Man Singh I, a great connoisseur of art. Man Singh is also reputed to have enjoyed cordial relations with the Mughal Emperor Akbar, another great patron of the arts. The enamelled golden crutch staff of the Maharaja remains one of the finest examples of enamel work and is unsurpassed in its brilliant usage of colours. It was under Man Singh's royal patronage that the five best enamellers were brought from Lahore to a workshop set up by the Maharaja, in Amber. The names of four of them—Zorawar, Jawahir, Sookha and Bharion, all belonging to the Sikh faith—are recorded in the royal archives of Jaipur. The tradition of their exquisite craft was passed down from generation to

JAIPUR ENAMELS

The Jaipur enamels stand supreme among the work turned out in India. They were, and are still occasionally, of matchless perfection. In *The Journal of Indian Art, Vol.1, 1886* it has been recorded: 'Perhaps the earliest known example of Jaipur enamel work is the crutch staff on which Maharaja Man Singh may have leaned as he stood before the throne of Emperor Akbar at the end of the sixteenth century.' It is described as 'fifty two inches in length, and (is) composed of thirty-three cylinders of gold arranged on a central core of strong copper, the whole being surmounted by a crutch of light-green jade set with gems. Each of the thirty-two upper cylinders is painted in enamel with figures of animal, landscapes, and flowers. The figures are boldly and carefully drawn by one who had evidently studied in the school of Nature; the colours are wonderfully pure and brilliant, and the work executed with more skill and evenness than anything we see at present day.'

A fine example of the Jaipur enameller's art.
Below: *In Jaipur, even the inner side of a lid was given the same attention that the main surface merited. (National Museum, New Delhi.)*

A round plate from Jaipur presented to King Edward VII when he visited India as the Prince of Wales, which took almost four years to craft is said to be the largest enamelled article ever produced.

Another superb example of the Jaipur enamellers' art was a writing case in the shape of an Indian gondola-like boat also presented to the

Prince of Wales. The stern of the small vessel is shaped like a peacock with its tail sweeping under half the length of the boat, studded with brilliant blue and green enamels, 'brighter even than the natural iridescence of a peacock's tail'. The canopy of the boat, which also covers the ink bottles, is resplendent in blue, green, ruby and coral-red enamels—is laid on the purest of gold.

An elephant goad (*ankus*) of the Maharaja of Jaipur was displayed at the Vienna Exhibition in 1883. Wilbraham Egerton says: 'The art of enamelling in other parts of India has not attained that perfection reached at Jaipur, but occasionally beautiful specimens may be found, as shown by the sheath of the Gorkha kukri, enamelled with flowers in brilliant colours on a blue ground exhibited in the Windsor Collection.'

The enamelling of Jaipur is executed on pure gold in the champlevé technique in which the metal sheet is engraved. The enamel is then applied on it, so that when it is fused, the lines created by carving disappear, and the entire surface becomes a sheet of translucent enamel.

In Jaipur, the furnace is sunk into the ground about a foot and a half deep with a channel below for air and supply of fuel. Over this is placed a thin layer of clay traversed by fine tubes for the air draught, and under this a small earthen vessel holding the 'glass' to be used for the making of the enamel colours. The colouring matter is added to the 'glass' when fired, and once cool it is ready for use.

The main features of Jaipur enamels are the translucent blue and green colours on the front of the ornaments, in which are set precious gems such as diamonds, emeralds and rubies in floral and foliage patterns in the *kundan* technique (a technique for setting gems in jewellery). The reverse side of the ornament is richly enamelled in polychrome enamels.

A modern copy of the peacock-shaped writing case presented to Edward VII when he visited India as the Prince of Wales.
Above: *Detail of a* hansuli *from Jaipur.*

Studded with diamonds and other precious stones and hung daintily with pearls, this kundan *collar was a favourite piece of ornament with many Rajasthani and Mughal princesses. The reverse side (see facing page), though hardly visible, was equally beautifully wrought. (National Museum, New Delhi.)*

This nineteenth-century necklace in the form of an enamelled collar, is studded with pearls and diamonds. It is a fine example of the famous enamelling work (meenakari) *done in Rajasthani kingdoms. (National Museum, New Delhi.)*

KUNDAN

Kundan is probably the oldest form of jewel crafting in India. Small pieces of pure gold are hammered into paper-thin sheets and encased around the gems to hold them in place. *Kundan* jewellery is very popular all over India but more so in the state of its origin—Rajasthan, where the main centres for *kundan* work are Jaipur and Bikaner. The jeweller inserts a gold foil between the gemstone and the metal base to give it a brilliant shine and lustre. Thus, in *kundan* work, the gem receives natural light only from above as the entire lower half is buried in the metal.

Kundan jewellery has many unique points that are worth noting. *Kundan* is not only crafted in twenty-four carat gold, but since the stones do not have a claw or open setting the craftsman can use gemstones that may not be all of a regular size or uniformity. Compared to open setting, this saves the craftsman time and labour as there are already grooves, and a gold band/case is placed around the gem. However, the stones retain their original look and distinctiveness. Again, the setting of stones in *kundan* does not require the gold to be heated as it is soft and pliable enough to set the gems by merely pressing them into the metal.

Nevertheless, the enamelling that goes into the making of *kundan* jewellery is a long and tedious process. First the design is made on the metal base. Next the engraver engraves the design with a sharp tool. Then the master enameller takes over the ornament and fills in the colour within the metal compartments. The whole item is then placed in the furnace for firing. When the finished item is ready it has the beauty and lustre of the finest quality.

A pink kundan *pendant from Benares.* Kundan *is probably the oldest form of jewellery crafting in India. Small pieces of pure gold are hammered into paper-thin sheets and encased around the gems to hold them in place.*

Right: A kundan
necklace on a string
of pearls is a twentieth-
century piece from
Delhi.
Far right: A jeweller
crafting a fine detail on
a piece of kundan.
Below: Kundan work
is almost always
embellished with fine
enamelling on the
reverse, as can be seen
from these bangles.

generation within the families of these craftsmen. Sardar Kudrat Singh was from one of the enamellers' families who had the distinction of being decorated with the *Padma Shri* (a National Award bestowed on Master craftsmen by the Government of India for outstanding work in a craft tradition).

The Jaipur craftsmen are specialists in white enamel work. The most popular motifs rendered on a white background are flowers, creepers and flowering plants. The white colour of Jaipur enamelware is sparkling in its clarity and with the combination of red poppy flowers with green leaves on the *safed zamin* (white surface), the resulting piece is amazing.

Wilbraham Egerton notes that while Chinese enamel is very rarely pure white, the ground of Jaipur work is usually a dazzling white.

Most of the pieces of the Mughal period were decorated with red poppy flowers and green foliage on a white background, probably adopted from the contemporary Deccani enamellers.

Ruby-red enamel on the surface of the pieces was another special feature of Jaipur enamellers. They excelled in this

to such an extent that later on, Jaipur and red enamel became synonymous. In fact, red flowers with yellow or white highlights are a hallmark of Jaipur enamel. Intricate designs with yellow, green, white and gold colours were produced on a radiant red background. Red enamelling on the front of ornaments studded with diamonds are, however, a rare collector's item.

Red and green flowers on a plain white ground derive from the white marble architecture of the first half of the seventh century, inlaid with flowers of jade and carnelian. These are copied on some of the finest goldsmiths' work to have been produced under Mughal patronage. These colours were by no means exclusive to Jaipur, and can be found on several eighteenth and nineteenth century pieces from jewellery centres as far apart as Murshidabad and the Deccan. *(The Golden Treasury.)*

Partajikam, or monochrome enamel, is another feature of Jaipur enamel. The pattern is chased on the gold surface and deep green coloured enamel is applied on it leaving behind fine gold lines. The design thus looks like gold scrolled across the unicoloured enamelled background.

This collection of
enamelled boxes in a
variety of styles and
shapes shows the rich
imaginative palette of
the Indian enameller.
The pink one (see left)
is an eighteenth-century
Mughal piece.
(National Museum,
New Delhi.)

ADORNMENTS FOR MEN AND WOMEN

Jewellery in India has traditionally been both an investment and a statement of status and prosperity. In India, the fine aesthetic sense of the rulers and their love of ornaments is responsible for the fact that men and women of all classes enjoy wearing dazzling jewellery. However, 'male' jewellery differs from 'female' ornaments. For instance, men wear necklaces, but these are heavier than the daintily-crafted necklaces worn by women. Men also wear earrings although they are not as elaborate as the ones worn by the women. Jewelled waist sashes and finger rings are also popular. A tiger's claw pendant, considered a lucky charm, and is often worn to ward off the evil

eye. However, the adornment of the turban is a royal prerogative and the turbans of the ruling elite are heavily encrusted with jewellery and fastened with a gem-studded aigrette. The *sarpech* or the turban crest worn in front of the turban has strings of pearls or bands of gold that extend from the front to the back of the turban. The ruling elite also held their weapons in great esteem and even scabbards, sheaths of daggers, hilts of swords and daggers were studded with gems or enamelled and then set with gems. The common man, however contented himself with silver jewellery with coloured glass in the place of gems.

Feminine jewellery is worn as a complete ensemble rather than randomly mixed and matched pieces. Royal ladies wore a lot of head ornaments each with a special name. Lotus-shaped gold chains were wore across the length of their braided hair and flower-shaped hair pins and combs that were magnificently enamelled and set with precious gems were also used. However, even village women in Rajasthan wear more than one necklace, earrings, finger rings, nose rings or studs, bangles of various styles, arm bands, anklets, toe rings, ornaments for the forehead, a round pendant (*borala* or *bodla*) that rests on the forehead held in place by a long chain of gold or silver or a string or pearls, hair ornaments, hair pins and many more smaller ornaments. Thus, when the ladies complete their toilette they are bedecked from head to foot in fine jewellery. Puzzled by the sheer number of ornaments worn by Rajasthani women, one can be forgiven for wondering how they carry such a load so happily.

Facing page: *The adornment of the turban was a royal prerogative. Called a* sarpech, *this is a particularly well-crafted* panchrangi kalgi.

Mughal thumb ring, enamelled in blue, black and white and set with precious stones, is an eighteenth-century piece (Victoria & Albert Museum, London). The elongated mount that points downwards, was meant to cover and protect the joint of the archer's thumb from injury.
Above: *A Mughal* nav-ratna *necklace, enamelled on the reverse, in the shape of a tiger's claw. (National Museum, New Delhi.)*

This late eighteenth-century nav-ratna *and gold amulet from the Mughal period, is set with nine precious stones and white sapphires. The reverse is finely enamelled with floral motifs and a traditional peacock. (National Museum, New Delhi.)*

Animal figures, such as elephants, deer, lions as well as birds, in bold floral motifs within a cartouche of round, oval, triangle, square and other shapes on a white background were greatly favoured by the artisans of this region. There are examples of a pair of pigeons or doves being executed within hexagonal or octagonal frames, the space around the figures was filled in with small flowers and green foliage on a white ground. Blue surfaces were decorated with red flowers, green leaves on a white background while the sky blue ground has foliage designs in red and green.

Beautiful figurative subjects are also a feature of Jaipur enamels. Opaque ground colours around the figures are used in contrast with the transparent enamel colour used for the motifs. In an example of this contrast work, Lord Krishna is shown narrating the *Bhagvad Gita* to Arjuna on the battlefield of *Kurukshetra* (the site of the battle in the epic *Mahabharata*) in the centre of the ornament. This central motif is surrounded by the ten avatars (*dashavataras*) of Vishnu, including Rama and Sita worshipped by Hanuman and Lord Jagannatha with his wife Subhadra and brother Balabhadra. Another example illustrates Rama and Sita seated on a *chowki* (low seat), flanked by Lakshmana (Rama's younger brother) and Hanuman. One necklace depicts figures of the nine planetary deities (*nava-grahas*) on their celestial mounts in polychrome enamel on a red field. A crude figure of Lord Shiva in blue is depicted seated on a yellow lion skin. His trident (*trishul*) is white and two types of flowers with leaves and buds are executed on the red field within the white border of the pendant. The figures of Radha and Krishna under a tree are depicted in red, yellow and green colours. However, the nine gems (*nav-ratnas*) were generally set on a green enamelled background. But in rare examples these are studded on a red ground (*lal zamin*).

Another feature of the enamel of Jaipur is the depiction of the same motif on the obverse and reverse sides. In some pendants, a spray of rubies and diamonds studded to depict flowers is shown on the front and the same motif is rendered on the back in white enamel on a red background. Another example has the symbol *Om* made of topaz on a red base on the obverse and the reverse is also decorated with the same design in white and red colours.

The pieces made during the Mughal period were enamelled with lotus and poppy flowers and green foliage. The flowers are made mostly of red and light pink while various shades of green from light to dark were used to illustrate the leaves and creepers. Doves, pigeons, swans, parrots, kingfishers and *bulbuls* (Pycnonotus Jocosus) were some popular bird forms of this period. In early Mughal pieces,

and till the mid-eighteenth century, there is no depiction of the peacock in enamels from Jaipur. It appears to have become a favourite subject of enamellers later.

Jaipur enamelling is done on brass and copper objects as well. Red, blue, white and mauve are used to decorate the metal surfaces. Enamelling on arms was also favoured and members of the Allah Baksh family continue the tradition of decorating hilts of swords with enamel. It is worth noting that the ancestors of Allah Baksh were brought to Jaipur to train the Jaipur royalty in the art of warfare.

Apart from Jaipur, Bikaner, Jodhpur, Udaipur and Nathdwara are other centres for enamelling in Rajasthan. The enamellers who migrated from Jaipur to these areas carried the art with them.

Left to right: An enamelled armlet (National Museum, New Delhi) depicts Radha and Krishna in a grove; a nineteenth-century pendant from Jaipur, delicately enamelled on the reverse, has Radha and Krishna on the front.

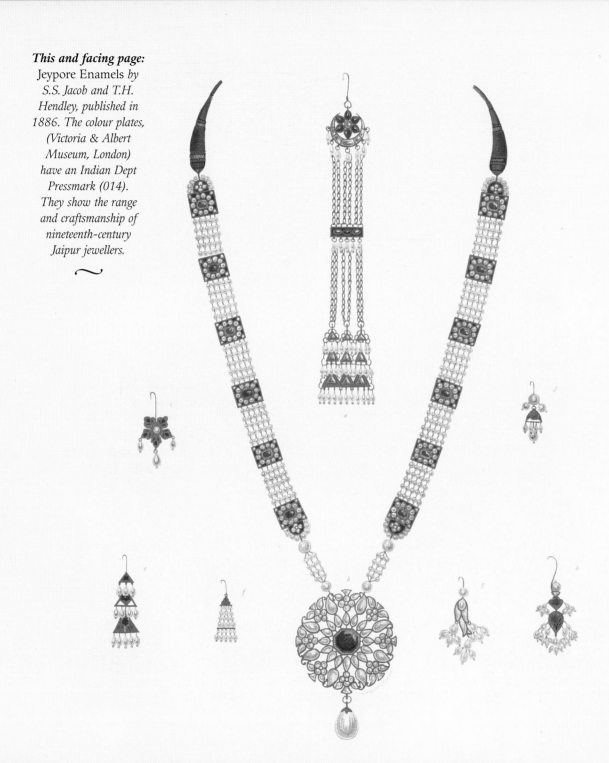

This and facing page:
Jeypore Enamels *by S.S. Jacob and T.H. Hendley, published in 1886. The colour plates, (Victoria & Albert Museum, London) have an Indian Dept Pressmark (014). They show the range and craftsmanship of nineteenth-century Jaipur jewellers.*

These eighteenth-century
bracelets are set with
diamonds and a ruby
in the centre, and
enamelled on the reverse
side. (National Museum,
New Delhi.)

~

THE DECCAN

~

Enamelling was patronized in certain centres in the Deccan even before the Mughal period. However, from the sixteenth century onwards enamelling spread widely over the subcontinent. A serious study of various types of enamels, their characteristics and peculiarities reveals trans-regional interrelationships.

The basic characteristic of Deccan enamel is the *safed chalwan* (white background) with motifs rendered in gold. This style of work resembles early *partajikam*. Often the white enamelling is done on a gold surface in the champlevé technique with the foliage pattern made of gold enamel. In some cases, red, blue and yellow flowers with golden stems or creepers are illustrated on a white field. Another feature is that diamonds, rubies and emeralds are set in the *kundan* technique on white enamelled surfaces.

Sometimes the surface is divided into different compartments of various shapes and the main motif, such as a flowering tree with three or five flowers with buds and leaves, is depicted on a white ground. The corners around the motif are filled by bird figures in white, blue and yellow enamel.

There are a few examples where the red surface of the object is decorated with a white flowering tree that has green leaves. In others, maroon fields are shown with white and blue birds with yellow beaks in pale green enclosures.

The Deccan is also famous for its green and gold enamelling. The

background is enamelled in a leaf-green colour while the floral and foliage designs are executed in gold, yellow and white colours. The green enamelled ground is provided with a full-blossomed, four-petalled, red-coloured flower with yellow pellets in the centre. Three petals are shown in the half-blossom floral design with white tips. The leaves and stems of these flowers are in yellow.

Some examples have bottle-green fields, which are painted with white, yellow and blue birds encircled with flowers and foliage depicted in white and blue shades. In some items, four varieties of flowers in different colours are presented on a single background. The petals of the flower range from four to eight. Birds are interspersed in the branches of the tree. The reverse sides of many ornaments are enamelled with floral patterns. Five-petalled lotus flowers with black pellets in the centre are surrounded by white enamel strokes and two green leaves.

Poppy flowers are generally depicted in a deep reddish-maroon colour and the white dots in the centre are painted over the maroon colour while green leaves are on a brilliant white background. In rare cases, when these flowers are depicted in red with white highlights on a turquoise ground, the stems and leaves are yellow in colour. There are examples which contain the floral and foliage design on a turquoise background.

Plants and floral motifs are also presented in monochrome enamel from the Deccan. The rich dark green colour and delicately executed flower heads and flowering trees are an important feature of Deccani enamel. A red flower with green leaves with yellow highlights on a white field suggests workmanship of an early period of Deccani enamels.

The coordination of green and blue and the bold treatment of the motifs is a striking characteristic of Deccani enamels. In one example, the flower motif is rendered in dark green and translucent green. A colour of unusual quality with dark blue, white and minuscule golden yellow highlights in the centre is another peculiarity of the Deccan. Floral motifs in red, green, powder blue and white

The basic characteristic of Deccani enamel is the white background (safed chalwan) with motifs rendered in gold. Often the white enamelling is done on a gold surface in the champlevé technique with the foliage pattern made of gold enamel. This Deccani piece with a strong European influence is the only one of its kind in the collection of the National Museum, New Delhi.

NAV-RATNA

The *Garuda Purana* ascribes the origin of gemstones to the slaying of the demon, Vala, whose severed limbs were transformed into precious gem seeds; his blood transmuted into rubies; his teeth became pearls, and so on. Each gem possessed characteristic powers of enchancing or controlling individual traits. Emeralds had positive influences on intellect and wit, diamonds were associated with inner and outer refinement, blue sapphires had to be used with caution as the influence of Saturn could often prove destructive. It was only when gem stones were combined in a unique manner with particular reference to the individuals that their beneficient effects were felt.

The setting of the *Nav-ratna* is determined by rules known to astrologers and jewellers. Patterns established according to the cardinal points were adopted, with individual variations determined by horoscopes.

The ancient Hindus attributed various qualities to precious stones. There are certain stones which could not be worn by themselves but only in conjunction with others.

The Mughals also came under the influence of Hindu superstition and had faith in astrology; they even consulted astrologers, before taking any important step. The hold was so great that even the fanatic Aurangzeb could not get rid of his belief in them.

Therefore *Nav-ratnas* are set in armlets, rings and amulets, purposely for their talismanic effect.

Nav-ratna jewellery became very popular with the Mughals and *Nav-ratna* necklaces and bracelets of huge uncut stones became typical of Muslim jewellery.

An eighteenth-century Mughal nav-ratna *necklace is strung with nine precious stones. (National Museum, New Delhi.)*
Facing page: *A* nav-ratna *piece of rare craftsmanship. (National Museum, New Delhi.)*

From left to right:
Called bazuband, *an armlet was worn by both men and women. These three pieces are from the collection of the National Museum, New Delhi. The first two pieces (left and centre) are in the typical Mughal style with a pair of birds in the centre, encircled by a floral pattern. The one on the far right is a particularly fine Mughal piece, from eighteenth-century Rajasthan. It is the reverse side of a* kundan *armlet depicting lotuses.*

on a surface is also typical of Deccani work.

Some Deccani pieces have two types of designs in enamelling on one object. Half the object is decorated with green and gold enamel work while the rest is furnished with floral pattern on red or green ground. White flowers with green leaves finely executed on a red field abound in the Deccan. In some pieces, eight-petalled flowers are perfectly positioned within the space with fillers of leaves and small flowers.

Rare Deccani specimens reveal another important feature of enamelling probably patterned on Bidri work. It highlights foliage and floral patterns rendered in black on a gold background.

Floral depiction in white on a sparkling red surface is yet another outstanding feature of Deccani enamel. The bold pattern of red flowers with white, green, blue or yellow centres and sometimes with golden yellow highlights with green or parrot green foliage on a white surface enhanced with areas of monochrome green and gold is a testimony to the high quality of Deccani enamel.

A three-dimensional effect is given to the Deccani motifs. In such cases, the surfaces are enamelled in red and green and are slightly above the surrounding field. In an outstanding example, the opaque white, blue, and pale green pattern is enamelled on a black background. This is a departure from the traditional Mughal palette of vibrant green, red and blue colours and points to obvious European design and influence.

Enamelling on silver is also done in the Deccan. Silver objects are gilded and the floral and foliage pattern rendered on the surface with blue and yellow flowers and leaves are depicted in a pale green or a bluish-green. In some cases, the grapevine is presented on the silver gilded grounds. The leaves are depicted in turquoise-green and the bunches of grapes are represented in light maroon colours. Blue buds with turquoise-green leaves, often support the pink and yellow flowers. Such a contrast enhanced the visual value of the object and is a speciality of Deccani enamelling.

Deccani enamelling was also used to decorate arms and armour. The iron hilts of daggers and swords were gilded in gold and decorated with yellow flowers with white pellet in the centre encircled with a red border on a green ground. In some pieces, red flowers with white stems and green leaves were displayed on a gold surface. The fronts of the sword hilts, harness fittings, lockets and chape of scabbards were enamelled mostly in green, but in a few cases in white and red as well. These were studded with diamonds, rubies and emeralds in *kundan* settings. In many cases, the iron hilts of daggers had a silver cover. These were enamelled in the champlevé technique with painted enamel. Flower designs were painted in white enamel, with yellow dots and green leaves in the centre.

Nav-ratnas (see pp. 42-43) are set on a turquoise enamelled field in the Deccan. It is interesting to note that all shades of green, ranging from rich dark green, pale green, leaf-green, parrot-green, water-green, bottle-green to turquoise-green have been used in Deccani enamel work.

Generally the motifs depicted in Deccani enamelling are flowers, foliage, birds, animals, creepers and trees. Chief among the flowers are poppy, lotus, jasmine, iris, marigold, rose, datura, narcissus and daffodils. The enamellers have also portrayed birds, such as swans, ducks, pigeons, cranes, doves and

Chand bali *earrings from Hyderabad shaped like a double crescent with a fish motif, set with uncut diamonds. The reverse is enamelled in red and green. (National Museum, New Delhi).*

parrots. Deccani enamellers also used patterns of leaves of different types extensively. Some examples of the leaves used in the process are—simple leaves, oblique leaves, falcate (sickle-type) leaves, long leaves (like maize leaves) and vine leaves.

In course of time, Deccani enamelling was confined to Hyderabad, when the Nizams of the Asaf Jahi Dynasty shifted their capital there. Enamellers from all over India flourished under their royal patronage so that every type of enamel technique can be viewed in the Nizams' jewel collection. Later, however, green and black enamel became distinctive of the Hyderabadi enamels.

BENARES

~

Benares (Varanasi) is one of the oldest cities of India with a rich history going back more than five thousand years. It is also one of the holiest Hindu pilgrim centres with several important temples and shrines dotting its crowded lanes. Since it draws pilgrims from all over India, it has become a popular place for the creation and sale of handicrafts.

By the seventeenth century, when the Mughal Emperor Jahangir shifted his administrative capital from Jaunpur to Benares, the city was already famous for its handicrafts. In 1750 AD, when Oudh was established as a state, Benares came under the reign of the Nawabs of Oudh (Awadh). Many artists and artisans were patronised by the Nawabs and a unique style of painted enamel work evolved here.

Gulabi meena (pink enamel) is the name popularly associated with this traditional style of enamelling, because it includes areas of painted enamel, which are generally translucent. Pink flowers are executed on an opaque white ground, although it is not difficult to find blue enamel used similarly. All other enamelled parts of the object are created in the champlevé technique, which makes this a mixed style of enamelling.

An immigrant Persian enameller introduced this style to the enamellers of Oudh in the seventeenth century, when the Mughal court was at its zenith. A similar type of enamelling was done at the Persian court at Isfahan, and the technique reached its perfection in Isfahan during the Qazar dynasty in 1795-1924. Many specimens of Qazar enamelled objects clearly demonstrate this. The Persians derived their inspiration from contemporary Europeans from glazed painting on porcelain and Swiss painted enamel watchcases of the seventeenth to the nineteenth century, which were popular in Persia.

It is also recorded that Kaiser Agha, an Afgan merchant (said to be from Kabul) visited Benares. He was well-versed in the art of pink enamelling, which he had learnt from Persian enamellers. He imparted this technique to the craftsmen of Benares. Gradually, this came to be known as rose enamel or *gulabi meena* (pink enamel) as the enamellers add a little rose oil to the enamel paste to bind the colour.

Benares enamellers first draw the outline of the design on the surface of the object and also follow the champlevé technique like the Jaipur enameller. They engrave all parts of the objects with parallel lines to receive the enamel and then start the application of enamel on the object. To create 'pink enamel' an object requires at least five separate enamel applications, with the object being fired each time to fuse the enamel on to the metal base.

In the first application of enamel, transparent blue and sometimes green colours are applied and fused on to the metal at the first firing. Then the exposed metal of the object is cleaned to remove the oxidation. The parts of the object meant for the next enamel application are then burnished, which increases their ability to reflect light through the transparent enamel.

The second filling of transparent enamel is done on the top of the first layer, to bring the enamel to the level of the metal. Other colours are applied

This nineteenth-century Benares enamel pendant has the signature pink work of this style and hangs from a necklace of precious beads.

The princely states of India are treasure houses of rare and beautiful works of art and artefacts. Among these, the foremost is the Nizam of Hyderabad's exquisite jewellery collection. Consisting of both his personal acquisitions and heirlooms of the Adil Shahi dynasty, it was created by master craftsmen from Persia and Hyderabad. The result is a near perfect blending of Islamic and Hindu art and culture. The collection also has jewels that display the best of Deccani Hindu craftsmanship and European styles of the eighteenth and nineteenth centuries.

With the decline of the Mughal Empire, some of the finest master craftsmen were attracted to the wealth and pomp of the Nizam's court in Hyderabad. An adjunct to the fabulous wealth

Kalgi Almas Parab, a turban plume, set in kundan *with black enamelling on the reverse, is a part of the Nizam's collection. Black enamel is rare and seldom seen on Mughal-style jewellery. Very fine enamelling in black was a hallmark of the Deccani craftsmen and often executed to contrast it with the sparkling diamonds on the front.*

of the Adil Shahi rulers were the fabled diamond mines of Golconda that yielded several gems that were made into pieces of jewellery. The enamelled pieces in the Nizam's collection, are among the finest pieces of their kind anywhere in the world.

Although there were different schools of enamelling, the enamels of Hyderabad continues to be gem-set on the front with exquisite enamelling on the reverse. Unfortunately, not enough scholarly attention has been paid to it even though some of the finest enamelling found in south India had its origin in Hyderabad. However, with examples attributed to Deccani enamelling the main features of the Deccani style jewellery have complex designs and elegant enamel detailing on gold, with the surface of the metal seldom being overcrowded. The thrust of the designs lies in flowers, nature and their various details. The colours used are deep, dark and rich with dainty touches of white.

Dinshah Gazdar in 1950, reported: 'I have never set eyes on such jewels before. Each piece is beautifully enamelled on the back in colours obtainable only after pounding precious stones. Today if I were asked to produce even a small replica of one of these I would be unable to do so, for these are unique specimens of a lost art.' In fact, they are considered so valuable that it is said that 'if they were put on the market all at once, they would wreck it.'

Sarpechs (turban ornaments), necklaces, rings, armlets, waist girdles, bangles, earrings, bracelets, *nav-ratna* buckles, *hanslis* (a solid one-piece necklace), brooches and countless other jewel-studded and enamelled pieces—all encrusted and fairly dripping with diamonds, pearls, rubies, emeralds and enamels, are to be found in the collection. Among them is also the Jacob diamond (which the Nizam reportedly used as a paper weight), a rock that weighs a stunning 184.50 carats and is counted among the largest of its kind in the world.

A unique feature of the Nizam's collection is its fusion of the two cultures of Hyderabad—Islamic and Hindu. These were amalgamated to produce a style that was and is distinct and exotic. Among the most striking examples of this work is a turban plume called *Kalgi Almas Parab* with its frontal showing a pear-shaped, table-cut diamond-set scroll surmounted with a huge drop pearl. The reverse of this piece is enamelled with black *mina* with an opening for a feather, and the

tapering stem to fix the ornament in a turban.

Black enamel is used very rarely and sparingly in traditional Mughal-style jewellery, because the technical expertise for such enamelling needs to be very high. That Deccani craftsmen had obviously obtained a level of skill required to make such piece with black enamel is clearly demonstrated by the fine black enamelling on this piece.

The Nizam's jewels are an exceptional collection in India and have been seldom seen in the three hundred-odd years of their existence. So great was the public interest generated by its air of mystery that poets and writers wrote of its legendary beauty out of imagination born of curiosity. Then, in 1972, the collection was offered for sale and after years of negotiations, it was finally acquired by the Government of India as the jewels were declared a part of the nation's heritage. When the collection was opened to the public for viewing, unprecedented crowds thronged the National Museum in New Delhi, where it was displayed for over a month.

Three traditional bracelets (kangan) *with elephant heads. A spring clip, cleverly concealed by the jeweller, allows the* kangan *to be slipped on and fastened securely.*

~

after the second filling, as this application is not possible earlier due to their hardness.

The next application is done with the opaque colours such as white, yellow, pistachio green and turquoise. These colours are applied more thickly as compared to the transparent colour. All enamels are fired and ground down to make them level with the metal. In the fourth filling, opaque white enamel is applied the second time only in those areas where enamel painting is executed over white. After firing, the transparent and opaque enamels are ground to bring out their smoothness and shine, although, the second coat of white enamel is not ground down to the level of the metal. These white areas are slightly raised to give the piece an interesting convex shape.

Pink (yellow and ultramarine colours) enamel is finely ground and mixed with rose *attar* (essential oil) and applied on the white ground with a fine painter's brush, with a tip made of the hair of the young squirrel's tail. This technique is similar to Indian gouache painting. The pink colour is not actually pink but red enamel, which is finely ground to a consistency devoid of any visible particles.

When the brushwork is complete, the object is given its fifth firing, also called *gulabi anch* or pink firing. For fusing the pink enamel to the white ground, quick and hot firing is done as in the case of red enamel. The enameller has to be a consummate artist, with the ability to reproduce his motifs, to create perfect flower and bird forms with delicate and sensitive outlines through fine engraving and

painting and graded application of the tints, to give a masterly effect.

Generally, lotus and rose and sometimes chrysanthemums are painted in pink on a white background. Relatively heavy outlines of flowers are drawn and the shades of each petal created with brush strokes from dark to pale pink to white. The colours remain darkest near the original line and lighten as the brush strokes move outwards. Doves and pigeons complement these floral motifs. Transparent ultramarine colour is used to paint the blue lotus with the centres of the flowers painted in yellow. Birds are also represented in the same way.

The front of bracelets is enamelled in translucent green colour and diamonds are set in between the grooves in the *kundan* technique. Heads of elephants are painted with three and five-petal lotuses in pink colour on a white field while bird forms such as doves, parrots and peacocks are executed in white, pink, blue and green colours.

In some cases, the floral motifs are painted in pink and yellow within a round frame and the space outside the border is enamelled in blue and decorated with foliage motifs. Another example illustrates three types of floral design in one object. The inner side contains a full-blossomed lotus with buds and green leaves, while the outer rim has a group of three half blossoms with two buds and green leaves.

In one necklace, the front side of each pendant has a painted figure of Srinathji in a glass cover within a border of white and pink enamel. The reverse side has flowering trees, roses and buds with green leaves and two birds. Each small pendant has one flower with two birds while the central pendant is decorated with a flowering tree with three rose blossoms, two buds and green leaves. Two birds are depicted on either side of the flower in the upper corners. A special multicoloured style of enamelling termed as *pachrangi meena* (five-colour enamel) is also noteworthy. Five colours—opaque and transparent white, transparent dark blue, transparent green and transparent red—are used to represent a decorated motif on a coloured surface of the object.

Enamelling on silver is also found in Benares. There are specimens where

The reverse side of a leaf-shaped gold pendant, enamelled in the distinctive style of Benares, depicts a hunting scene.

This kundan *necklace,
shimmering with white
topazes, is now in
the collection of the
National Museum,
New Delhi.*

The reverse side of the same Benarasi necklace, exquisitely enamelled in pink, rivals the glory of the topazes on the front.

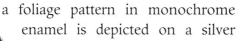

a foliage pattern in monochrome enamel is depicted on a silver background. This work is similar to *partajikam*. Many enamellers produced decorated enamelled objects of silver in polychrome enamel, which is done in the champlevé technique with painted enamel.

The pink enamelling of Benares continued for a period of a hundred and fifty years and ended in the early twentieth century when master craftsman Babu Singh died in 1923. Now barely a handful of enamellers produce enamelled jewellery in Benares. A few craftsmen work with silver to produce purely decorative objects for the national and international market. Sadly, the pink enamelled jewellery of Benares is more or less a lost art.

LUCKNOW

~

This nineteenth-century pendant with floral motifs has the famous pink enamel for which Benares was famous.

~

Another important centre of enamelling in North India was Lucknow. The State of Oudh was established in 1750, when Nawab Wazir of Oudh Asaf-ud-Daulah

transferred his capital from Faizabad to Lucknow. Lucknow till that time was a small town, which developed under the Nawab to become one of the foremost cities of the north. No court in the country could match the glory of Oudh, a state where Asaf-ud-Daulah had under his royal benefaction distinguished artists, musicians, poets and writers. Many artists, craftsmen, traders and merchants came to his capital to live and work under his royal patronage.

The court of Oudh, at Faizabad until 1775 when it moved to Lucknow, had by the mid-seventh century established its own style of vibrant translucent blue and green enamelling on silver.

Though the use of silver is somewhat unusual, the champlevé technique is the one used in all enamelling, except for the Iranian-derived painted example. A magnificent *huqqa* (hookah), one belonging to Robert Clive and in a 1766 inventory, is probably Oudh work.' (Robert Skelton *et al., Treasures from India, The Clive Collections at Powis Castle*.)

The craftsmen of Oudh developed a style of enamelling in which they drew the outline of the pattern by using dyes on the surface of the object. Its main feature is a pattern etched on silver, covered with green and blue with a small patch of yellow and brown enamel. The pattern is minutely drawn and overflows with design and colour, so much so that when the object is viewed from a distance, it appears to be corroded with verdures (a green or bluish patina formed on copper). The dominant colours used to depict the foliage patterns are green and blue, while brown and yellow colours are usually used in animal forms.

Floral designs in pink enamel were also a feature of the State, probably introduced by Benares craftsmen who had relocated to Lucknow. There is no background colour on the metal surface. The absence of a well-marked scheme of colour composition places this style of enamelling as inferior in artistic merit to other schools of enamelling. The surfaces are laden to an astonishing extent with foliage and animal figures. Fish forms are also prominent in this work. Flowers, foliage and vine leaf designs are popular motifs in Lucknow enamel work.

In some examples, sword hilts are covered with intricate designs and large surfaces of silver are left exposed. The pattern is in a graceful scroll with glazed blue flowers and green leaves that are rendered in an orange or pale turquoise blue shade. Modern forms of birds abound too with fanciful circular tails of peacocks. Peacocks, long-tailed birds and floral motifs are sometimes executed in oval medallions.

The peculiarity of this enamelling is that the pattern is overburdened with forms and figures but it is clearly drawn and the spacing between the forms is attractive. Another speciality of this enamel is the green flowers with blue centres and white highlights. Apart from the traditionally used colours, the enamellers of Lucknow experimented with two or three shades. In one example, white flowers with orange centres, yellow stems and pale green leaves are depicted on a bluish green field.

Objects decorated with enamel in a considerable range of colours on silver are generally identified as Lucknow enamelware. Mostly clear, cool blue and green colour enamels are used on silver while in Jaipur enamel, the enamellers used gold as a metal base. The effect of translucent enamels on silver often gives the item a luminosity

A hunting scene adorns this pendant.

A late eighteenth-century piece, this enamelled box with a cover in silver and gilt, is from Lucknow. (Victoria & Albert Museum, London.)

and freshness. The designs of Lucknow enamels are an all-over pattern depicting hunting scenes while the depiction of fauna covers a wide range. The designs are enriched with floral and foliage motifs. However, the emphasis is not on forms.

In Lucknow enamels, the designs are realistic but generally lack in composition. On closer examination animal, birds and human figures are seen dispersed over a floral surface. However, the main defect of the style is the absence of main decorative lines to fix and guide observation.

Lucknow and Rampur are also important sites for producing articles with an etched design on silver, in which blue and green enamels predominate with small areas in yellow and brown. In some very rare specimens produced in Lucknow, some objects are decorated with black enamel-like bidri ware.

The nineteenth century, pieces made for an exhibition from 1851 onwards and now in the Victoria & Albert Museum, London, show that blue and green were still the keynote colours, but that a soft, pale, translucent violet and the slightly harsh, opaque gamboges yellow had been added, together with both opaque and translucent turquoise. (Stronge, Smith and Harle.)

RAMPUR

The State of Rampur (near Delhi) was also an important centre of enamelling. The enamelling done in Rampur was very similar to that of Lucknow, often making it very difficult to differentiate the lineage between the pieces. The style of Rampur enamelling is quite bold and effective when compared to the Lucknow enamels. Blue and green colours are mainly used in representing the designs and the spaces between the sub-divisions are well defined.

THAPPA WORK

In the ordinary way of making ornaments the metal is first melted down and then given the desired shape by hammering the soft pliable metal. However this technique is employed for the manufacture of ornaments that are solid. In the manufacture of hollow ornaments the two halves of the piece are made separately and then joined together. In the case of designed ornaments pieces of the molten metal are put on *thappas* or dies. The metal is then hammered till the metal takes on the desired shape of the ornament to be made. The smaller details of the item are made separately and fused to the main piece. The whole ornament is fired again for a little while and then polished. It is finally given to the engraver who is a master of engraving minute designs which are later enamelled. The finished product is lustrous and beautiful to look at.

Two gold pendants from the first century BC, believed to be inspired by Roman designs. Such pieces go back to a time when there was a flourishing sea-trade between Rome and India. The gold armlet, studded with a red stone, and with bird, animal and floral motifs, is from the nineteenth century AD.

Displayed at the Great Exhibition held in 1851 in London's Crystal Palace, this silver gilt spice box set with crystals is from Rajasthan. It is now in the Indian jewellery collection of the Victoria & Albert Museum, London.

Gold floral designs set against a brilliant blue enamel background make this nineteenth-century box and cover from Kashmir a collector's item. It is now in the Indian jewellery collection of the Victoria & Albert Museum, London.

⁓

One fine example is a beautiful flowering tree with blue flowers executed on a metal surface in blue and green enamel. The flowers are in blue and the leaves, in green. Another example displays white and green enamel in a floral design on an opaque enamelled background. Another fine example is a hookah base with a beautiful floral and foliage design on plain background within a border. The remaining space is covered with a foliage pattern all over in blue and green colours. Some pieces have an etched design filled with two colours applied thickly, which appear from a distance as if corroded.

KUTCH

Kutch and other areas of Gujrat in western India were famous for decorative enamels, which contained floral motifs on silver in low relief. Silversmiths of Kutch were famous all over India for their decoration on arms in repoussé work. The enamellers of Kutch attained a high degree of proficiency in their craft under the royal patronage of this princely state.

In the enamelware of Kutch, the outline of the design is stamped on the object to be enamelled and the whole surface is then uniformly covered with enamel, leaving only the faintest lines of gold, so that the pattern looks like cloisonné work. The enamel is then fused on to the metal surface making the whole design redolent of the embroidery of Kutch. The enamel work of this area surpasses all the outstanding specimens produced in the entire subcontinent and rivals the finest enamelling of Europe.

In one example, flowers are painted with blue, yellow and pink coloured enamel, while the leaves are depicted in a golden colour on a green background. In a pair of finger rings, the pink and yellow flowers are painted on a green enamelled surface. These two specimens suggest that the colour green is usually used only on the surfaces of the objects. Of all the various colours available only two colours of enamel were popular with Kutch enamellers for the flowers—pink and yellow. The expertise of the craftsmen is undoubted in rendering the glazed coating of enamel on the surfaces of the object to ensure uniformity, firmness and durability. Painting of fusible colours created the shading in the flower petals. However, unlike the Jaipur enamels, their colour lacked depth and transparency. Enamellers today decorate boxes, trays, etc., in the cloisonné technique.

MULTAN
~

Enamel work flourished in Multan, now in Pakistan, in the nineteenth century and came to an end after the partition of the subcontinent when the enamellers migrated to India. A similar type of work was being done in Kangra, Himachal Pradesh, and in Hoshiarpur Punjab. In early examples, the artisan created the design by engraving as in the champlevé technique but later on, hammering the *thappa* or dies onto silver plaques produced patterns. The patterns were stamped on the objects in Bahawalpur, Pakistan, and then brought to Multan for enamelling. Depressions were created on the object by the hammering of dies onto the metal surface to provide space for filling the enamel colours. This gave the object a special look and provided an overall uniformity to the design.

An enamelled pen-box (kalamdaan) from Kutch, in west India, done in the cloisonné technique. (National Museum, New Delhi.)
~

Rustam J. Mehta writes: 'At Multan, a short cut method used to be practised, probably still is, especially for large production of trinkets like brooches, buttons, studs, etc. Instead of producing the depressed areas of designs in which enamel is laid by graving out, the design is engraved on a steel die or *thappa* into which the silver plate of trinket being made is beaten to produce thin raised lines, almost mechanically, the enamels are laid and finally fired.'

According to the jewellers of Multan copper is added to silver because the alloy makes the metal resist the heat of fire better.

In Multan, silver ornaments are enamelled in red, black and a poor yellow, but these are inferior specimens as compared to those of Jaipur and Delhi.

Many enamelled objects like bowls, cups, glasses, plates and different types of small boxes and containers were produced in Multan. Generally, the design appears in line in the base metal while the background is in one colour enamel. In some cases, when figurative motifs,

geometrical patterns and floral designs are made, the forms are filled with different colours of enamel to set them apart from the background colour.

The metal used in Multan enamelware is an alloy of silver and copper in equal proportions. This alloy conducts heat better for fusing the enamel on to the metal. After the first firing, the enamel is ground to the level of the metal pattern and re-fired to bring out its brilliance.

Opaque enamels were used in the background. The predominant colours were deep blue and lapis lazuli. Other colours such as green, black, red, pink, yellow and white were also used but to a lesser extent when elaborate patterns were made on the object, in order to highlight the piece. Finger rings, toe-rings, pendants, buckles, bracelets and buttons were also made as enamelled jewellery in Multan. Unfortunately, the craft is extinct today.

SINDH

The enamelware of Sindh resembles the enamelling done in Punjab and Rajasthan but in Sindh, the champlevé technique was more popular. In some Sindh pieces red, white, green and

blue enamels are used to execute the design, although enamellers sometimes imparted a single beautiful olive brown or green shade to the gold object.

In one example, enamelling is rendered in pink and green colours on a white and brown wavy surface depicting lotuses of four different types with green leaves and birds in different postures using the champlevé and painted techniques. This object itself is unique and rare.

Another object is decorated with three different motifs on a green and golden yellow background. The flowers are executed in a white colour with light blue centres on a yellow ground and flowering plants with yellow flowers with light blue dots on white centres rendered on a green surface, and each flowering plant is depicted within a frame. Blue lotuses are depicted between each flowering tree. The lowermost part is decorated with light blue lotuses with blue

centres with three white and light blue dots on top of the blue centre. The birds in the design are depicted in white while the leaves are shown in green enamel.

'Iranian enamelling (was) also found at Hyderabad under the Talpar rulers of Sindh: here the influence was direct, Iranian masters merely carrying out their work under a different patron. The colours are much more vivid than those of Benares, with yellows and oranges vibrating against pink. Even there, however, a softer, more 'pink' style seems to have evolved, judging by the signed and dated enamelled dagger and scabbard, which appeared on the art market in 1987.' (Stronge, Smith and Harle.)

BAHAWALPUR

~

Bahawalpur was a centre known for its enamelling on gold, with the

Facing page and *above:* Moulds for making jewellery in different shapes. These examples are found primarily in South India.

~

enamellers showcasing their skill through the use of transparent and opaque enamels. In this style, the patterns are large and significant, executed on an enamelled background. The spacing in between the motifs in gold lends to its uniqueness.

In some cases the enamellers raised the motifs on the coloured surface by a thin drop of opaque white enamel called 'slip'. This enamel work very closely resembles Chinese copper enamelled vases, plates and cups. Large-sized objects such as finger bowls, cups and vases were produced in Bahawalpur. Rich deep blue mixed with green has mostly been used in highlighting the pattern on the objects. In Bahawalpur, a translucent blue enamel is mostly used.

Bold motifs depicted in the colour blue in some vases are very attractive. A rare piece with raised blue flowers in a combination of either a white or red centre illustrated on a dark green background is an outstanding example of this style. T.N. Mukherji records that 'Bahawalpur makes a peculiar kind of silver vessel, called "Mokhaba". It is a covered dish which is highly ornamented with chasing, enamelling, and gilding.' The designs are mainly floral, geometrical diaper or scroll, the general effect being rich and attractive.

HIMACHAL PRADESH

In Himachal Pradesh enamelling is mostly done on silver. Floral and geometrical patterns are made in green and blue colours in the local champlevé technique. Sometimes the silver objects are gilded with gold and when the enamel is heated the mercury volatilizes, leaving a dull effect on the surface, which is polished by rubbing the surface with an agate or steel burnisher.

Usually, the silver jewellery of Himachal Pradesh depicts four-petalled blue flowers with green pellets in the centre and two green leaves. In some cases, the four-petalled floral design is surmounted with a small half-blossomed flower. Flower buds are also depicted in blue and green colours.

Another motif represented in Himachali jewellery is a flowering tree supported by two birds in enamel. Sometimes a small flowering tree is depicted on the silver surface in a blue colour. Figures of deities are also depicted in some jewellery pieces. In such cases, Vishnu, Ganesh, Shiva or Durga are seen within a border while the central figure is always depicted surrounded by floral motifs on three sides. This type of representation is generally found on pendants.

Chanderseni haar is a necklace popular in some parts of the state. This is an ornament that, traditionally, is worn during the wedding ceremony by the bride and this tradition is still very much in evidence today. The necklace is worn not just by the Kinnauri women but by the women in the Kulu region of Himachal Pradesh as well. The *Chanderseni haar* has a stylized lotus flower as the central design and is flanked by flowers on either side within a double-lined border in the central pendant and terminals.

Three types of borders are used in the jewellery of Himachal Pradesh. In some parts of the State, crude enamelling in blue and yellow colour is made on the design blocked by dies. This resembles the enamelling of Multan. According to J.L. Kipling, 'At the closing of the century, the silversmiths of Kangra are skilful in the application of vitreous enamel to small articles of silver used as ornaments. Finger and toe-rings, necklaces in great variety, ornaments for brow, head and ears connected by chains are decorated in dark blue and green enamel. The patterns sometimes include figures. An old Kangra pattern of anklet now seldom made is a series of birds of very archaic design in enamelled silver, connected by silver links.'

In Kangra light blue colour enamel was also used sometimes. In one rare specimen, now in the collection in the National Museum, New Delhi, rubies and emeralds are set on the light background on the front side.

Kipling observes: 'Red and yellow are not so often seen, and the colours, though true vitreous enamel, are opaque. It might be described as champlevé in so far as that the enamel is laid in hollows between raised lines

The craftsmen of Kashmir have worked with metal from time immemorial. Kshemendra, a philosopher, and Kalhan, poet and author of the poem *Rajtarangani*, testify that kings and nobles used to dine off dishes and cups of gold and silver. The use of gold by Muslim rulers has been alluded to. They also used certain types of silverware including hookah bases, spittoons and water sprinklers.

Enamelling was once a flourishing craft in Kashmir. Beautiful goblets with long cylindrical necks and graceful handles, dishes, teapots were all delicately engraved with motifs taken from nature and enamelled in soft tones, which gave a brocade-like effect to the precious metals.

Kashmir work, with the surfaces of the objects being covered with floral and scroll designs with one colour enamel, seems to bear a Persian influence. There is a minor difference

*A nineteenth-century gold nose-ring (*nath*) from Himachal Pradesh inlaid with semi-precious stones.*
***Facing page:** This nineteenth-century rose-water sprinkler from Lucknow, (Victoria & Albert Museum, London), is cast in silver and enamelled in gold and green. The cup and saucer, a modern piece, depict the famous Hawa Mahal of Jaipur. (National Museum, New Delhi.)*
~

of metal. These are, however, produced by hammering the silver plaque into a steel *thappa* or die and not by graving out.'

Although the enamelling of the past was noteworthy for its beauty and durability the current enamelling on jewellery is of a very inferior quality because the craftsmen mix the colours with ready-made synthetic adhesive and apply it on a ready-made stamped design firing it only a few times. The end product is thus fragile as a finished product as the enamel flakes off with just a slight rub.

in the enamelling technique used here. For example, in Kashmir the design is repoussèd on the objects whereas in many other centres it is engraved.

Birdwood has mentioned: 'Among the Prince of Wales' presents are several specimens of charming Cashmere enamels, in which the ground of the usual shawl pattern ornamentation, cut in gold is filled with turquoise blue, perfectly harmonized by the gold, and producing a severely artistic effect.'

The chinar leaf motif is very popular with Kashmiri craftsmen and is also used profusely in embroidery. This design is still the mainstay of Kashmiri shawls and textiles.

The best forms of enamelled arms such as hilts of the daggers, handles of the swords were also produced in Kashmir.

Kashmir was also one of the centres of making the base metal articles in imitation of precious enamelled ware.

The metals used for enamelling in Kashmir are—silver, copper and brass—the work on the latter two being inferior to that on silver. The pattern is punched or repoussèd on the metal surface to make it ready for enamelling. Kashmir enamellers favoured a

light blue colour in their work, and embedded or filled in the depressions, or the metallic surface of the object with easily fusible paints. After this the object was fired at the appropriate degree of heat to fuse the enamel on to the metal surface. This brought out the colour in the finished form.

Instead of gilding the copper, the Kashmir silversmiths sometimes plate the base metal with silver or tin before enamelling. On copper objects, different shades of blue are most frequently used, while a shade of light blue enamel is applied on brass. Enamelling done on brass is coarser— although it is not translucent—and does not crack easily. However, it loses its brilliance with the ageing of the metal.

A gold spoon, of Mughal origin, enamelled with delicate green and red enamel work. (Victoria & Albert Museum, London.)

～

Various distinctive styles and patterns were in use of which the following have been enumerated by George Watt and Percy Brown: 'The Arabic style, which consists of elongated flamboyant figures that convey an impression of being composed of Arabic inscriptions. When closely examined the pattern seems to be a geometrical, complex design of bifurcated and minutely interlaced floral scrolls. Traditional shawl patterns have also been adopted in enamelling objects. The pattern ornamentation is cut into the metal surface and is filled in with turquoise blue. Sometimes a dark green is intermixed with blue. It is perfectly harmonized with the gold and produces a most artistic effect. The floral rosettes on a black background, consisting of numerous small rosettes assorted on a spiral twisted line, which passes all round the object form an intricate pattern.'

In some objects the Western influence is evident. The typically traditional chinar pattern is highlighted against a dark background. In Kashmir painted enamelling is executed in an embossed technique, with the pattern being raised. The objects made of other alloys like white metal were coloured with lac, with colours being introduced to form flowers and rosettes with leaves. According to J.L. Kipling in 1884 in the *Journal of Indian Art*, 'Though colours are somewhat crude and the enamel is applied with more boldness than delicacy, the general effect is undoubtedly bright and attractive.'

An enamelled plate in the Sri Pratap Singh Museum in Srinagar represents a unique style of enamelling that is different from the style of enamelling usually done in Kashmir. It displays Shiva and Parvati being worshipped by a king or a noble and resembles a miniature painting of the Persian style. This is the only example of its kind available in India.

Kashmir enamel may be described as an intermediate between the fine enamel work of Jaipur, Delhi and Benares and the lac-coloured ware of Moradabad. The art of enamelling, it seems, would have a good scope of revival though, as with the skill that Kashmiri craftsmen possess, it should be possible to make some attractive modern objects and designs using this technique.

DELHI

~

Delhi became the centre of enamelling when craftsmen from Jaipur migrated to Delhi. Delhi being the seat of the Mughal Empire, craftsmen from all over the country also came here to produce and display their best products. It is no wonder then that, over time, all manners of enamelling came to be available in Delhi.

It was Bansidhar, the son of Prithviraj Singh, a commander in the army of Humayun, who was responsible for the advent of enamelling in Delhi. It is an interesting point of reference that Bansidhar's son Mahabatrai was an acclaimed enameller. A gold shield was an outstanding work in enamel produced by him for the Maharaja of Punjab and is considered to be the most rare example of this craft. The sons of Mahabatrai—Ramjidas, Shyamlal, Totaram and Kanhaiya Lal—were also experts in this art. Later, they moved to Jaipur.

Early examples of Delhi enamel work are currently on display in the National Museum, New Delhi. The speciality of Delhi enamel work is its white background with floral and foliage patterns rendered in red, green and blue colours. However, the white colour is not as dazzlingly clear as that found in Jaipur enamels.

There is one enamelled plate of brass with the portrait of Emperor Humayun in the centre, which has been attributed by

These exquisite nineteenth-century lockets from Jaipur showcase the fine craftsmanship of that region. The front of these pieces are studded with diamonds, while dainty enamelling decorates the reverse side. Both these are now in the Indian jewellery collection of the Victoria & Albert Museum, London.

~

MODERN ENAMELLING

Most big jewellers' shops offer an extensive range of enamelled jewellery. The Indian jeweller has at his fingertips all the tricks of the trade—inserting coloured tinfoil under cabochon-cut stones in the *kundan* setting to give an illusion of the depth of colour and the substitution of recent enamel as a genuine seventeenth-century article. Knowledge of the quality of enamel of the various periods will be of great help in the choice of a good enamelled piece.

The nineteenth-century enamel lacks finish and details. Though bold, the design is not well executed and the colours lack the exquisite brilliance and lasting quality of the Mughal period pieces and are liable to be chipped.

Most modern enamel pieces seem a pale parody of the old art. There are still workmen with a good sense of design but the colours of modern enamelware lack the translucent brilliance of the earlier work and look like ordinary painted metal. The outlines of the designs of the ill-finished recent enamel pieces are blurred and the colour tends to overflow the edges of the grooves. Even when freshly executed, the colours are likely to be

There are still workmen with a good sense of design but the colours of modern enamelware lack the translucent brilliance of the older pieces (see the parrot, National Museum, New Delhi) and often look like ordinary painted metal.

smudged or chipped. Where the design is intricate, modern enamel stands out from the older one by the purity of the latter's colour.

The older a piece (till the seventeenth century) the more intricate the design and the more brilliant its colours. A few recent pieces with enamelled deities or mythological scenes that are passed off as old, should be examined very carefully for minuteness of detail in order to to determine their real age.

The best enamelling is done on the purest gold. 18-20 carat gold does not take colours so well and does not lend itself to delicate designs, so its outlines are apt to be blurred. The quality of the gold too can, therefore, be judged from the quality of the enamel. Most enamelled ornaments are hollow and filled inside with shellac. A glimpse of its colour only in certain *karas* and *kangans*

(types of bangles) may reveal the proportion of the gold to the lac. Lac inserted in ornaments is of two kinds—*pachra* and *surmai*. *Pachra* lac is reddish brown in colour and is light in weight. *Surmai*, which is lead wax, is blackish in colour and is very heavy. If an ornament has *pachra* lac it will have more gold content in proportion to its total weight than if it is filled with *surmai* lac. If it is not possible, however, to find out the colour of the lac used, the proportion of gold in old ornaments may be safely estimated at five-eighth of its total weight. In more recent ornaments, the proportion will be less while in very recent ornaments gold can only be one-fourth of the total weight.

A head ornament worn on the forehead (tika), *this late eighteenth-century piece with Mughal motifs, is set with diamonds, emeralds and pearls. (National Museum, New Delhi.)*

The reverse of the same piece is daintily enamelled in a riot of colours and floral designs. Indeed, it is more colourful than the main side.

A buckle (baksua), *studded with rubies, diamonds, emeralds and spinels, this is from the early eighteenth-century, Deccan. (National Museum, New Delhi.)*

Jamila Brij Bhushan in her book *India Metal Ware* as the work of Moradabad, but the workmanship is of Delhi during the British rule in India.

Another interesting characteristic is the deep green, translucent enamelling on the ground, decorated with white flowers with yellow centres and stems. Another item displays white flowers with blue leaves and gold stems rendered on a red field. However, compared to the red colour of Jaipur enamelware, which is sparkling, this is a dull red with a yellowish tinge.

The depiction of one motif on both sides is another speciality of Delhi enamels. In a few ornaments, the peacock or a flower is depicted studded with diamonds and pearls on a coloured enamel background on the front with a similar design executed in red, blue and green colours on a white ground on the reverse. Floral patterns in gold enamel on a red background, as well as the use of a light blue colour in contrast with deep blue, is another feature of Delhi enamels. The former can be compared to enamelware from *partajikam*.

PUNJAB

In many towns of Punjab a style of enamelling that was prevalent in the nineteenth century was executed with the design being created on the objects using the repoussé technique. In this technique, the deep depressions were filled with dark blue enamel, which gave a strikingly rich effect to the ornamentation.

The enamelling of Multan and Punjab is very similar, because both regions follow the same technique. Many enamelled pieces with the shawl pattern produced in Punjab were also similar to Kashmir enamelware. Before the partition of 1947, Lahore was the main trading centre for enamels. Enamel products made in Lahore were predominantly blue in colour. In Lahore, the ornament is deeply repousséd and the depressed areas thickly filled with rich blue enamel, which gives a brilliant decorative effect. Some of these splendid examples are preserved in the Lahore Museum.

The enamelware of Lahore is so far only known from the rather inferior work on the backs of the 'Order of Merit' introduced by Ranjit Singh, in emulation of the French Legion d'Honneur worn by one of his military advisors. (Stronge, Smith and Harle.)

An exquisite example of nineteenth-century meenakari *work from Rajasthan, this gold and enamelled bracelet is set with diamonds on the front. The reverse side (visible on the outer edges) displays the famous Jaipur technique of enamelling birds and floral designs in red and green on a chaste white background. It is now in the Indian jewellery collection of the Victoria & Albert Museum, London.*

An early nineteenth-century hooped Chand bali *in* kundan *work, set with diamonds and enamelled on the reverse side. Intricate fish designs hung with pearls, form the lower half of this Hyderabadi piece. (National Museum, New Delhi.)*

The poppy flower motif (which is derived from Jahangir's tomb) was also favoured by the enamellers of Lahore.

After Independence in 1947 Amritsar emerged as another market for enamel for jewellers from north India. The pieces were decorated with flowers and foliage patterns. Sometimes bird motifs were also chased on the objects. Mainly blue, green and occasionally red and yellow coloured enamels were used to highlight the pattern. Presently, enamelling is mainly done on rings and pendants, with the depiction of the names and figures of deities in black, blue and green colours.

ASSAM

The north-eastern part of India also followed a tradition of enamelling. It was also done on some ornaments in Jorhat in Assam. Strikingly beautiful effects are achieved on bracelets, lockets, earrings and necklaces by using blue, white and green enamels.

TECHNIQUES OF ENAMELLING

Facing page and *above: Front and back of an enamelled* hansli *from Rajasthan with a soft, lace-like effect. The rigid* hansli *tapers towards the end in the form of a collar necklace. The name of this piece is taken from the Indian word for collar bone,* hansuli, *on which it rests.*
(Victoria & Albert Museum, London.)

Enamelled container with lid, popular in the work of the Rampur region, this uses the champlevé technique. (National Museum, New Delhi.)

Like most Indian handicrafts, the art and secrets of enamelling are handed down from father to son of a special caste, which was traditionally presumed to have descended from divine ancestors.

Enamel is a vitreous coating fused on to a metallic surface. The top layer in the technique of enamelling is very simply a sort of transparent, colourless or coloured soft glass, created by the fusion of flint or sand, red lead and soda or potash called 'flux'. Metallic oxides are mixed with flux to get the desired colour of enamels. Two to three per cent of metallic oxide is added to the molten flux to get the proper colour—potassium chromate for yellow, manganese carbonate for violets, cobalt oxide for blues, copper oxide for greens and red iron oxides for browns. White enamel is made from antimonite of potash, iron oxide, and zinc carbonate with glass. The molten coloured material is mixed carefully and poured in the form of cakes. These cakes are broken up and ground to obtain a fine powder, which is washed thoroughly and applied on the object to be enamelled; the object is then fired in a furnace until the enamel fuses on to the metal base.

Although there are many different procedures of enamelling, the earliest technique of enamelling is cloisonné, in which separate compartments or enclosures are made with metal strips. Each enclosure is filled with a mass of powdered enamel. To ensure and prevent chances of the enamel cracking in the front, it is better to apply the enamel on the back as well. The reason enamel cracks is because of the differential rates of cooling between metal and glass. The plate attached to the back of the object is ideally one that has a slight curve in the centre with its edges turned downwards. The curved plate protects the enamel from contact with the iron plate on which the piece is placed while firing;

otherwise the enamel on the object may be damaged. Rotating a burnisher many times around the metal plate about 1.5 centimetres from the edge until the centre is raised creates the curve on the back plate.

The outline of the design is first incised into the surface with a steel point. Pieces of annealed wire, one centimetre thick, are used to make cloisons around it. The back plate is cleaned and each cloison is fastened with borax mixed with a little gum (tragacanth). The solder used is usually a mixture of four parts of silver and one part of copper. Japanese enamellers fasten the cloisons with a paste or gum and start to fill them immediately with enamel. When the object is fired, it holds the cloisons firmly. However, it is a good idea to solder down at least the principal divisions, taking extraordinary care to stop the solder from spreading over the ground lest it affects the colour.

The solders are then covered with rouge or whiting before each firing. After soldering, the object is boiled in a chemical solution to remove the borax and other waste material. The background and cloisons are then thoroughly rubbed, to emerge clear and clean, taking care that the fingers do not touch them. If the object is left unattended for some time, it should be kept in a covered vessel containing distilled water.

The cloisons' panel is kept face down on a blotting paper, and another coat of enamel is applied all over it with a spatula. Pressing a layer of blotting paper on it dries the enamel. The plate is turned over and loose cloisons are firmly stuck down with a little gum. Each cell is carefully filled with enamel taking care to spread it evenly into all the corners along the sides of the recesses. When all the cells are filled satisfactorily, the object is ready for the furnace.

The object is then placed on an absolutely level sheet of iron or nickel in the furnace. This plate is perforated, thus allowing the heat to penetrate easily to the back of the enamel. Sometimes this plate is also coated with rouge, whiting or plaster of Paris. A little gum or borax is added to these coats to prevent their breaking up.

When both the object and the plate are completely dry they are placed within the furnace. If steam rises from it, it is considered an indication that it is not ready for firing. Again, if any enamel should fall off, the object is immediately taken out and kept in a cool place. The enamel is then repaired and readied when absolutely free of moisture and put back in the furnace without shaking it. It takes from a few seconds to a few minutes for the enamel to fuse on to the metal.

After fusion, the powdered enamel shrinks to occupy less space than before and so may not completely cover the compartments. In such cases, those parts are scraped, cleaned and again tightly packed with enamel. For a second or subsequent firings, the plate is heated till it is red-hot. After the initial firing, it is taken out and repositioned in the furnace when the furnace is a little cooler. The slow cooling leaves the enamel nicely annealed, and ensures that there will be no crumbling of the enamel later.

The object is then held under cold running water and the enamel is ground down with a corundum stick— never with an ordinary file—to the level of the surrounding metal. This ensures that the enamelled objects will have a smooth, unpolished surface.

The surface is then polished with water and a fine corundum stick, followed by rubbing it with water and an Ayr stone, a fine-grained stone used for polishing marble, also called snake stone. This is followed by polishing with crocus powder on a strip of leather, and finally, with rouge and wash-leather. This lengthy procedure ensures a brilliant surface and brings out the precious quality of the enamel.

The polishing of enamel smoothens the metal, and if there are any empty spaces left from which the enamel is missing, there is a possibility of engraving a light pattern on these spaces. This will help to fuse the enamel and metal halves of the object aesthetically together. In some Chinese and other opaque enamels, the object is treated with an eggshell polish, which renders the enamel stunningly beautiful. Sometimes the metal parts of enamelled copper objects are gilded. If gilded by the mercury process, the enamel remains unharmed. Other- wise, the shock of a

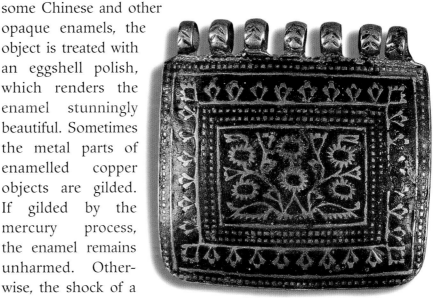

ROYALS AND JEWELLERY

The royal treasuries of the Indian princely States were the envy of collectors all over the world. Although the Nizam of Hyderabad's collection (see pp. 48-49) is believed to be one of its kind in the world, there were other royal treasures in India that were as spectacular. The jewels of the Jaipur royal family were hidden in the Jaigarh fort and guarded by the fierce Mina tribe. No one, it is said, not even the custodians, had any idea of the worth of this royal hoard. A maharaja was allowed to see this treasure trove only once in his lifetime and could select one piece. Other princely States famous for their jewels were the Maharajas of Patiala, the Gaekwars of Baroda and the Wodeyars of Mysore. The Maharaja of Patiala once sent a casket of jewels from his collection to the House of Cartier in Paris to redesign them into more modern pieces. Among them was a diamond that weighed a staggering 234.69 carats. It was the largest commission Cartier had ever handled.

The Indian princes were flamboyant and loved to display their treasures on their person. Their turbans were festooned with ropes of pearls and diamonds sparkled on aigrettes. Their necks were hung with pearls, diamonds, emeralds and rubies and their arms sported armlets. Even their swords and scabbards were like pieces of jewellery.

Royal turban ornaments and necklace (National Museum, New Delhi). Turban ornaments were worn by male rulers; their consorts had other ways of turning heads.

The late Duchess of Windsor once bought an Indian emerald drop necklace, re-made from an anklet of the Baroda collection from a famous dealer in 1957. Sadly, she decided to wear it a grand reception where the Maharani of Baroda was also present. 'My dear,' the Maharani said to her companion in a rather loud voice, 'do you notice, she is wearing the beads I used to have on my feet!' Seething at her humiliation, the Duchess apparently returned the necklace to the dealer the next day.

This sword and scabbard (Victoria & Albert Museum, London), is exquisitely damascened and enamelled. The Indian maharajas were fond of lavishing their arms and armour with such flamboyant touches.

The front and back of an enamelled Mughal armlet, in the champlevé technique. (National Museum, New Delhi.)

sudden temperature change may cause the enamel to crumble. To keep the enamel safe from damage, enamelled objects should not be put in a hot gilding solution.

The cloisonné technique is in existence in China and Japan. The Japanese also practise the art of enamelling. The pattern is often roughly painted on the background metal. It is then outlined with fine copper or gold in imitation of cloisonné enamels. The fusing of the colours follows as usual. A technique similar to the cloisonné technique is also in vogue with a few enamellers of the Kutch region of Gujarat in India.

Plique-à-jour enamelling is a sub-division of the cloisonné technique. It resembles miniature stained-glass creations. This type of enamelling has no metal background: the lead lines in the windows are represented by the metal cloisons made of wire in enamel. A filigree pattern is made on the metal surface to hold the enamel. Sometimes, it is made from a thick sheet of metal pierced with holes of suitable shapes. Then, U-shaped iron wire clamps are fastened down temporarily on to a sheet of aluminium, bronze or mica, because enamel will not stick to it. This process will also keep the back of an object clean and smooth after firing. The wires are tied or clamped down to prevent movement, while filling them with enamel. After baking, the colours of the enamels are translucent and create a stained-glass effect.

The champlevé technique of enamelling is practised almost all over India. Enamels are fused into grooves, which are carved, stamped or cast on the metal surface with a chasing tool. The goldsmith prepares the basic form from gold. Then he hands it over to the artist-designer (*chitera*), who draws the outline of the pattern on the surface using a needle with a sharp point. The patterned surface is rubbed with an agate burnisher to make the outlines stand out. The object is then ready for the touch of the engraver (*thathera* or *gharia*) who fixes it on a shellac stick, which is nothing but a flat, or circular wooden disc with a handle attached under it. Shellac is spread over the working surface and heated to make it flexible and the object is pressed on to it. On cooling, it becomes hard and holds the object fast. The carving is done within the outlines of the design with assorted and appropriate engraving tools, some of which have flat cutting ends while others are round based or v-shaped.

The *Ain-i-Akbari* (a record of the life and times of Emperor Akbar) contains a description of the technical skill of the Hindu goldsmiths. 'Each was practised by a specialist craftsmen, which meant that an engraved, enamelled and gem-set gold object would be passed from one to another in the royal *karkhana* or workshop, before being complete.' (Stronge, Smith and Harle.)

Of all the procedures of enamelling, the champlevé technique is beset with the most difficulties, the main one being, no solder should be present on the surface, as in the cloisonné technique. Otherwise, the solder may melt and flow onto the areas holding the enamel, when it is heated for fusion. These problems are

avoided in this technique because a border of exposed substrate metal separates each figure in the design. The entire space within the engraved outline is etched with a series of equal lines with a V-shaped tool. Etching helps the enamel to stick to the metal and prevents the enamel from flaking off. Besides, the etching will also diffuse and reflect the light back through the

Therefore, it is imperative that the object must have a level and well-polished surface. The object in this technique is enamelled on both sides. The forms on the surface below are clearly visible and the gradations in the height of the relief are reflected by variations in the colour of the enamels above it. Being translucent, all details of the modelling of the faces, the

transparent enamel thus increasing its colour, lustre and intensity.

The Bassetaille method is a subdivision of the champlevé technique. In this method, a level topped layer of enamel is fused over a design in low relief. The figures are first chased on the object and then are touched up by considerable engraving. Much of the effect of enamelling depends upon the modelling of the metal below it.

hands and the folds of the dresses and other details are thus visible through the enamel. The deeper the depression, the richer is the tone than in their shallower environs. To give a high-quality effect to enamel, the objects are carefully annealed by being allowed to remain in the furnace as it cools down.

Encrusted enamelling is another way of applying enamel to decorate the irregular surfaces of objects, such as the sides of finger rings, gold mounts of crystal cups, sword hilts and scabbards. Indian and Persian craftsmen followed this technique to ornament the surfaces of objects used by army personnel. The colours created by this technique glow so brightly on gold and silver that the value of the object is greatly enhanced.

The variety of such enamelled jewellery also suggests that the object needs support during its firing and fusion of the enamel. In small pieces the solders are covered with rouge or whiting, while in large elaborate works it is necessary to provide a cover of plaster of Paris. Large portions of the objects are covered with a mixture of plaster of Paris except those surfaces that are to be enamelled.

Encrusted enamelling is also executed on the figures in high relief created by repoussé work or chasing. This type of work is also found on some of the sixteenth-century jewelled book covers, made from plates of gold and silver. The designs are minutely created on these plates by the repoussé technique and then richly enamelled.

In the painted enamel technique, the surface to be enamelled is painted. Enamels are provided with a plain foundation sheet that is slightly domed in shape. The design is first outlined on a sheet of metal, which is slightly curved in the centre. This sheet is kept in a cold chemical solution, made of one part sulphuric acid and twenty parts of water, for an hour or boiled in that solution. Then both the sides are vigorously scrubbed with a nailbrush, using pumice powder and water. Wet enamels are applied on the surfaces in uniform thickness. The entire surface of the object is thus covered with enamel on both sides, as in the case of colours applied on canvas. Different colours are filled into the design with precision with successive colours applied when the preceding colours are dry. Colours of the same hardness are mixed together and spread all over equally and dried off with clean blotting paper before firing.

The enamels will be more brilliant—golden or

A richly-worked huqqa *base from Lucknow, in the champlevé technique.*
(National Museum, New Delhi.)

Another huqqa *base, again from the Rampur-Lucknow area, is also executed in the champlevé technique. (National Museum, New Delhi.)*

This aftaba, *a ritual water pot from Kashmir, is one of the finest examples of painted enamel. (National Museum, New Delhi.)*

coppery—if the copper surfaces are given a coating of clear flux (glass), depending on the composition of the flux and the temperature at which it was fused. Gold devices are stamped out in low relief on the enamelled surface. Motifs in gold are also painted on the enamelled background. Chinese colours are also used for enamelling. Chinese colours are basically mineral oxides with flux. Therefore, these colours must be provided with a thin film of soft flux to protect them from the effects of being exposed to the atmosphere.

During the sixteenth century, a large amount of work was done in grisaille (painting in shades of grey) on blue or black ground. This kind of enamelling can be found in India (Kashmir) where the craftsmen make objects using the painted enamelling technique. The copper surface is first covered all over with a dark-coloured ground. Then the designs were painted in monochrome with successive layers of white enamel. The shading, that emerges from the dark ground shows through the white enamels.

Whatever be the technique of enamelling, the coarser the enamel, the more brilliant it is, when fired. Having said this, one should add that

if the enamel were very coarse grained, it would not cover the metal fully nor fill the narrow spaces satisfactorily. Also when it is melted, it will retain air bubbles. Another problem that may arise would be that the uncovered part of the metal surface will become oxidized or a hollow may appear on the surface of the enamel when fired. In the case of copper that spot will turn black. Hence, care must be taken to ensure that the enamel is ground as coarse as the size of silver sand. Needless to say, absolute cleanliness is imperative if the best results are desired.

A detail of the aftaba.

THEVA WORK

*Theva work was practised only at Partabgarh in Rajasthan in western India
and so took no permanent foothold elsewhere in India. These two boxes
are now in the collection of the National Museum, New Delhi.*

This box and lid decorated with theva *work, is from Partabgarh. (National Museum, New Delhi.)*

∾

The princely States of Rajasthan have always been treasure houses of the arts. Situated in the district of Chitorgarh, in the south of Rajasthan, Deolia-Partabgarh is one such principality. Bordering Mewar, Malwa and Bagar, Deolia-Partabgarh was founded in 1561 by Bika, a young prince from the royal house of Mewar who moved to this area evidently seeking to carve an independent niche for himself. Emperor Shah Jahan awarded him the title of Maharawat Partab Singh; thus Partabgarh was named after him at the beginning of the eighteenth century. He laid the foundations of his small kingdom there by defeating the reigning tribal ruler, Queen Devi Mini. Later, due to the shortage of drinking water here, he relocated the people of Deolia to his new capital in Partabgarh, situated about eighteen kilometres to the east. In the year 1818, Partabgarh passed under the control of the British.

Today, Partabgarh is a small-fortified town with a population of about fifty thousand. It stands surrounded by the villages of the Bhil and Mina tribes. The economy of this state flourishes on a near-barter system of transactions between the money-lending Banias and Bora shopkeepers.

The Partabgarh craftsmen, who call themselves Raj Sonis, are the originators of *theva* work, a unique technique which originated approximately seven generations ago with Nathuni Sonewalla, a goldsmith relative of the present extended family of craftsmen who still produce *theva* work. He is said to have created this style of work in 1767, during the reign of the Maharawat Samant Singh of Partabgarh, under whose patronage he flourished. The source of his inspiration, however, remains unclear, as the process is similar to no other technique practised in India. At present, there are only four renowned families of goldsmiths in Partabgarh who carry on with this tradition.

An exquisitely detailed
photo-frame from
Partabgarh, this piece
is one of the finest
examples of theva work.
The figures (see details,
right), taken from
mythology, show
Lakshmi, the goddess
of wealth, Balkrishna
or child Krishna, Lord
Shiva in meditation and
Hanuman, the monkey
god, carrying a mace.
(National Museum,
New Delhi.)

~

As with all established traditional skills, the technique and knowledge of executing *theva* work passed from father to son, who start learning it at a tender age. The craft reached its pinnacle during Victorian times, when an important Western market had developed. Many *theva* objects set in gold were sold to British women living in or visiting the country and were subsequently taken to Europe as souvenirs where the work was recognised by European jewellery historians for its fineness and distinction.

The local name for this technique is *theva*, which in Rajasthani means 'setting'. *Theva* work was practised only at this location in India and so took no permanent foothold elsewhere in India. T.N. Mukherji of the Indian Museum in Kolkata in the late nineteenth century and Sir George Watt, Director of the Comprehensive Exhibition and the *Catalogue of Indian Art at Delhi*, 1903, recorded that it was also done at Ratlam and Indore in Madhya Pradesh, cities just across the present State border from Partabgarh in Rajasthan, but it is unknown in these places today. What seems likely is that members of Partabgarh families who had migrated there, possibly due to marriage alliances, practised it in regions apart from Partabgarh. Its concentration in Partabgarh, as so often happens with specialist crafts in India, is due to the fact that the craftsmen successfully hid their techniques from outsiders.

In the last quarter of the eighteenth century, the craftsmen of Partabgarh reversed the use of materials in enamel work and produced a similar but monochromatic effect with gold leaf appearing on etched glass. This technique is known as *theva* (meaning 'setting' of enamel or quasi-enamel work. *Theva* work is also known as Partabgarh work).

The craft of theva *reached its pinnacle during Victorian times, when an important Western market had developed. The bracelet and necklace on these pages are part of a set now in the National Museum, New Delhi.*

This craft was erroneously described as a form of enamelling in the late nineteenth and early twentieth centuries. *Theva* work does not resemble enamelling either in appearance or in technique even though it looks similar to enamelware at first glance.

Enamel, which is a glass-like substance, is applied in a granular or powdered form to a metal ground to which it is permanently fused by heating. The reverse takes place in *theva* work in which a thin gold-foil sheet is heat-fused to the visible surface of an already existing sheet of glass.

Another difference lies in the way light is reflected through enamel and *theva* glass. Indian transparent enamel is done over a substrate of precious metal engraved with a linear pattern that helps to hold the enamel and reflects light through the enamel layer above it. In the case of transparent *theva* glass, light is reflected from a separate sheet of metal foil placed below the physically separate *theva* glass unit. The latter method is also used when setting gemstones in traditional closed-setting Indian jewellery, and this is the source of the practice in *theva* work. This is also possibly the reason for the choice of a separate word—*theva*—given to this art. *Theva*, however, emphasizes the comparable traditional method of stone-setting and has no reference to the technique used to make a *theva* plaque, as one might expect. Perhaps even the designation was deliberately ambiguous.

Nowhere else in India does this skill and fine expertise exist—elsewhere the effect of enamelling emerges by fusing the coloured substances on to gold or silver or other metals, whereas in *theva* work it is done only on glass. In 1965 five families practised *theva* work in Partabgarh. Beniram Mathuralal, Ramprasad Ramaljee, Ramvilas, Mathuralal and Shankarlal Mathuralal were outstanding craftsmen, who described the technique to the author of *The Traditional Jewellery of India*.

According to Sir George Watt, 'the article is made of a piece of green- or red-coloured glass, or a thick layer of enamel, the crude material for which is imported from Kashmir.' He goes on to say: 'a frame of silver wire, of the exact size and shape of the glass, is next made, and across this is attached a sheet of fairly thick gold leaf. This is then embedded on lac and the pattern punched out and chased on the gold. The glass is then semi-fused, and while still hot the rim of silver and film of gold are slipped over the edge and pressed on to the surface of the glass. The article is again heated until a sort of fusion takes place and the gold and glass become securely united. Before mounting the article, a piece of silver tin-foil is placed underneath the glass to give it brilliancy.'

Thus, *theva* work can be described as fusion appliqué of a pierced patterned work sheet of gold foil, which is transferred on to transparent coloured glass. The piece of glass is encased in a frame of silver or metal wire. The colours of the glass pieces are usually red, green and blue, and can be round, oval, and drop-shaped, square, rectangular or octagonal in shape, with the largest dimension not exceeding six centimetres or so.

The design is minutely punched out on a twenty-four carat *sone-ki-chadar* (gold sheet). Different sheets of blank foils are fixed side-by-side, one after the other on the work surface, which is a board covered with a layer of lac. The lac is heated and the metal sheet is pressed tightly and firmly into it. When the lac cools down, it hardens and holds the metal down while it is being worked upon.

Traditional designs are carefully outlined on the gold surface with a pointed steel scriber. The designs fall into two main groups—mythological or religious and secular.

Some popular subjects among the former are Lord Shrinathji, Radha-Krishna, and Lord Krishna with the *gopis* in *Ras-Lila* (a divine dance of the Krishna legend), Rama *darbar* (court) and Hanuman, and Shiva-Parvati. Secular subjects are—*shikargah* (a hunting scene) depicting animals in the jungle replete with foliage, huts and domestic animals, scenes with horses and scenes of battle. Special subjects such as portraits were also made if these were commissioned.

The designs of theva *jewellery fall into two main groups—those with mythological or religious themes and those with secular ones. (Victoria & Albert Museum, London.)*

Now in the Indian jewellery collection of the Victoria & Albert Museum, London, this dainty nineteenth century necklace has pendants of theva work crafted in Partabgarh, Rajasthan. Each piece depicts figures of various Indian gods and goddesses.

~

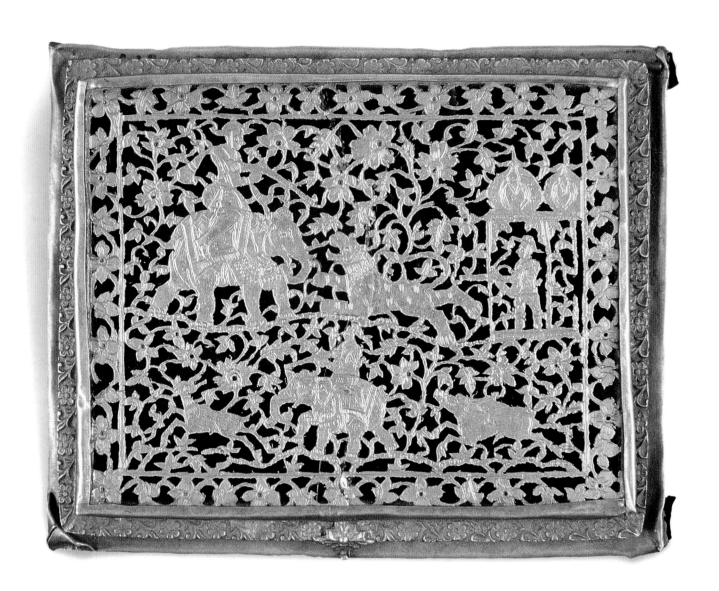

One of the most beautiful and finest examples of *theva* work is a plate about thirty centimetres in diameter. It has a central circle surrounded by concentric circles of lotus petals. In the centre is Maharana Pratap holding a javelin in his hand, astride his famous steed Chetak. Each of the four lotus petals in the concentric circles around this image depict him in different situations. In one he is shown with his chief queen. The second petal shows him with his minister, Bhama Shah. In the third petal he is shown in a pitched battle between the Maharana and Salim. The fourth depicts a moving incident between two brothers: the Maharana's brother Shakti Singh, deserting the army of his ally, the Mughal army, to help his brother when he sees the latter in dire distress on the battlefield. Thus each petal recreates a historical event in minute and vivid detail. The next concentric circle is a relief from the petals charged with historical events, and depicts sixteen beautiful winged fairies—eight dancing and eight playing music. The final circle of petals presents vignettes of the pleasures of court life: a coronation scene, a royal procession, the king granting an audience to his ministers, a royal hunting scene, the worship of the family deity, a royal wedding, the pleasures of married life, a foray into the forest, the birth of a prince and the attendant festivities, village life in Mewar, a battle scene and the installation of the Pillar of Victory.

Details within the subjects are created with small punches, since each unit has different shapes and patterns, such as straight and curved lines, circles, dots and textures. The punches are held vertically over the desired spot and lightly tapped with a small metal rod. A very light pressure is enough to impart an impression on the gold foil. Leaving the surrounding frame intact, the entire internal background of the design is then removed by piercing, through which the coloured glass is seen.

The finished *theva-ki-patti* (pierced work sheet) is heated and peeled off from the lac surface, cleaned and dried. The extra metal outside the design frame is trimmed and finally the

A pair of dainty earrings with peacocks and flowers, these are now in the National Museum, New Delhi.
Facing page: *Theva work was popular among European clients. This box shows a hunting scene (shikargah) with exotic Indian animals in a jungle. The hunters, however, are British, judging from the hats worn by them. Often such pieces were made as special commissions for important British clients. (National Museum, New Delhi.)*

small pieces of gold are removed from the background.

A completely clean glass is placed on a sheet of mica since glass will not stick to it when warmed. The finished gold sheet is laid on top of this. The glass and gold sheet are transferred to a small, open, clay crucible, which is filled nearly to the top with sand and ashes. An open hearth with glowing charcoal is prepared and the open crucible with long 'U' shaped tongs is placed on it. The *theva* piece remains visible and exposed to the air in the open crucible. The craftsman uses a long brass blowpipe to maintain the temperature in order to fuse the metal to glass. He watches the condition of the glass constantly, in order to judge its state of fusion. As soon as the glass becomes red hot, the metal is fused on to the glass surface. The glass piece is then allowed to cool slowly to keep the glass stress-free. If the glass cools too quickly, it might crack later due to internal stress caused by the differential rates of shrinkage of glass and metal. Since the gold used is pure twenty-four carat, no discolouration takes place on the surface in oxide forms during the heating. This could happen if it were a gold alloy containing copper.

The goldsmith then mounts the finished unit into a specially prepared frame. To enhance the colour and brilliance of glass, a flat sheet of polished tin foil is placed in the closed back setting below the *theva* unit. This reflects high light through the glass. Craftsmen use pure silver or tin foil under green, blue and red glass. In the past, yellow glass, which was painted red, was sometimes used.

In most of the objects, the *bazel* (rim/groove holding the gem or glass) metal is a silver alloy above ninety per cent in purity—commonly referred to as *shudh chandi* (pure silver). After placing the unit in its setting, the upward standing collar edges of the rims are turned down over the unit with a burnisher, to hold it in place, conceal and protect the edges. Since the setting is closed and baked, the foil inside is permanently sealed against direct exposure to the atmosphere and so it does not oxidize easily and remains untarnished for a long time. Sometimes the silver setting is gold-plated to harmonize with the gold-foiled *theva* unit.

According to Sir George Watt, the glass sheets came from Kashmir. Of course, the craftsmen claimed that they came from Germany! Due to restrictions on import, bubble-free sheets manufactured in Firozabad, Uttar Pradesh, are now used. Goldsmiths of the twentieth century, who worked with *theva* craftsmen, sometimes prepared elaborate settings in gold wire in Cantille style, with tight coils of gold in the shape of small flowers and foliage.

Many goldsmiths became cognizant of contemporary European jewellery styles and technology because they had the opportunity to see and handle imported pieces, which they could then copy with ease. In the nineteenth century brooches, buttons, cuff-links, hairpins and earrings with *theva* work were made for Europeans. Traditional objects, such as trays, cigarette cases, flower vases, visiting card boxes, which were decorated with *theva* units were also created. These units were also set into fans, umbrella handles, perfume bottles, photo frames and jewellery boxes, and it became a status symbol to own such beautiful items. Europeans frequently brought jewellery for Indian artists to copy. It is unlikely that un-mounted *theva* units were brought to Europe for mounting or that they were remounted by taking them out of Indian settings. It is true, however, that in India *theva* units were mounted as a backing in some Jaipur and Benares enamelled jewellery, but such examples are rare. In some cases, the front of the unit was set with stones and the back with *theva* work.

Some *theva* units were also used to mount or as a backing for enamelled jewellery from Jaipur and

Theva *work bracelet pieces from Partabgarh.*
Facing page:
An elegant hexagonal goblet in theva *from Partabgarh. Both these are in the collection of the National Museum, New Delhi.*

Benares. A few objects had gemstones on the front and *theva* pieces at the back. The finest examples of this craft have been preserved in several museums of the country and abroad. An extraordinary set of jewellery inlaid with *theva* units is in the Metropolitan Museum, New York. The Geological Museum in London has a large plaque, while an intricate

used in these examples is a shade of blue.

The jewellery made in the nineteenth century was mainly for the use of the European clientele, evident because their forms follow contemporary European jewellery fashions. The Indian buyers of *theva* work preferred to buy and wear belts, necklaces, and pendants representing

casket with marvellous narrative panels is in the royal jewel collection of the Queen of England.

Jewellery with *theva* units in gilded silver is still made in Partabgarh. However *theva* work was also done at Ratlam and Indore in Madhya Pradesh as recorded by T.N. Mukherji and George Watt. The prominent colour

traditional Hindu
subjects and generally did not use or purchase brooches, buttons, cuff links, hairpins, and earrings with *theva* work using European designs and patterns. Many of the items decorated with *theva* work that did not fall into the jewellery category were made in traditional Indian forms such as *thals* (trays)

pandans (containers of betel leaves, arecanuts and other ingredients) and *gulabdans* (rosewater sprinklers), but other forms such as cigarette boxes, calling-card boxes, and flower vases were made specifically for Europeans. Many forms, including swords, fans, and umbrella handles, shields, *guldastas* (flower vases), spoons, perfume bottles, jewel boxes and cigarette cases were produced and *theva* units were incorporated in the trappings of elephants, camels and horses.

Today the most popular forms of *theva* jewellery include hair pins, chokers, earrings, lockets, cuff links, watch chains, coat buttons, tunic buttons, rings, belts, various boxes, *choras dibbi*, a box to hold the image of the Jain deity Chanda Prabhu, which is always kept under a *dhakkan* (cover); and *tashak* (large round plates) used for *pan supari,* spices used in preparing a betel leaf.

Unfortunately, as only a handful of craftsmen are left in this area of work, this fine art is slowly dying out. However, the few representations that remain still evoke the memory of a rich and creative past when skill was recognized and creativity nurtured.

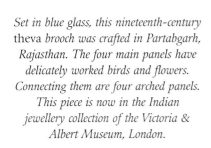

Set in blue glass, this nineteenth-century theva *brooch was crafted in Partabgarh, Rajasthan. The four main panels have delicately worked birds and flowers. Connecting them are four arched panels. This piece is now in the Indian jewellery collection of the Victoria & Albert Museum, London.*

INLAY WORK

*Two jade pendants with gold inlay work, showing a branch of a tree made of dark
green sapphire with buds and flowers made of rubies. These Mughal period
ornaments are now in the Salar Jung Museum, Hyderabad.*

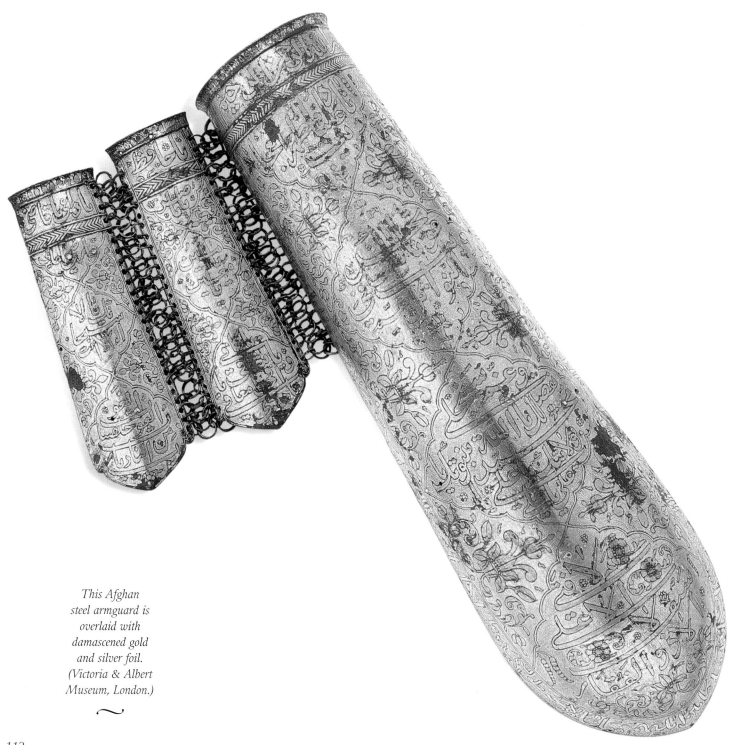

This Afghan steel armguard is overlaid with damascened gold and silver foil. (Victoria & Albert Museum, London.)

Inlay work is the decoration of a metallic surface using wire and pieces of gold or silver within the engraved or chased pattern. Although, inlay work looks very similar to enamelling it is quite different in its method of execution. In fact, on many an occasion it is considered as being enamelware though the technique followed for inlay work is completely different. Inlay work is implemented by using ivory, gemstones, semi-precious stones, gold or silver wire and small pieces of metal on to wood, marble and jade. Inlay work also includes damascening and bidri work as the inlay of wire and small pieces using precious metals is also a part of these crafts. This is why damascening and bidri work at first glance do have a striking similarity with enamelware.

DAMASCENE

Damascene is the art of encrusting one metal on another. The metal crusts are not soldered on or wedged into the metal surface to which they are applied, but applied in the form of a wire. It is thoroughly incorporated into the metal surface, which it is intended to decorate, by undercutting and hammering. Practically, damascening is limited to the encrusting of gold wire, although sometimes, silver wire was also inlaid on the surface of iron, steel or bronze. This system of ornamentation is peculiarly oriental in its origin and takes its name from Damascus. Damascening tasted its greatest success in Persia and Spain during the Ottoman period.

Exquisitely damascened
Mughal sword hilts.
(National Museum,
New Delhi.)

In India, damascening or *koftgari* in gold is done in Kashmir, Gujarat and Sialkot (now in Pakistan) and in the Nizam's territory. In this technique the design is chased on the metal surface with a hard and sharp stylus. The wire is held down with one hand within the grooves, while the craftsman hammers it with the other till it unites with the background. It is possible that this art had its origins in the ornamentation of swords and other weapons. Till the beginning of the twentieth century the craftsmen used to damascene the handles of swords, daggers, scabbards, shields and helmets. The art of damascening sword handles attained a high degree of proficiency in Jaipur, Alwar, Datia, Jodhpur and Sirohi. Intricate and elaborate patterns mostly done in silver on steel were produced in the damascening of Jaipur. Similar work was also done in Datia and Jodhpur. In the north, after the decline of the Sikh kingdoms, the damascene craftsmen of Sialkot and Gujarat turned their attention to making articles of domestic use.

According to Rustam J. Mehta, 'The art of damascening apparently arose with the desire of the soldiers of old to possess weapons of war that were decorative and ornamental as well as functional. And the craftsmen of those days must have been kept very busy damascening swords and daggers, shields and sheaths. It is well known that Emperor Akbar was fascinated by this art and himself supervised the work in his Royal Armoury'.

During the reign of Emperor Akbar the inlayers of steel were ranked equal to the inlayers of hard stones. According to Akbar's minister and historian, Abu'l-Fazl, they were designated *Zar-nishan* and received the same level of pay as craftsmen of precious-material work.

The finest work of the Mughal era is executed in inlay, in which grooves forming the lines of the design are cut so as to leave gripping configurations in the cavities. The precious metal was then hammered into these and locked into place. This technique appears to have been practised with special finesse in the Deccan.

Manuel Keen writes, 'The so-called "Oriental" arms and armour are legendary for damascening, a term used to refer to both the inlay and the overlay of steel with precious-metal decoration (usually gold). In such embellishment, as with other aspects of arts and crafts in general and with other disciplines connected with iron and steel in particular, India excelled

Kundan inlay work was popular in the eighteenth and nineteenth century. It started as an art form in Delhi and its surrounding areas and developed as a craft of inlaying hard surfaces like jade with gold wire and precious and semi-precious stones. (National Museum, New Delhi.)

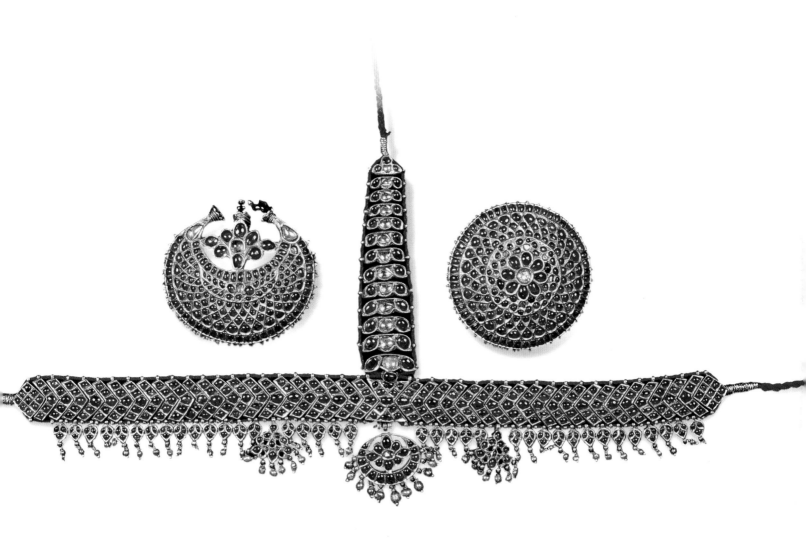

An eighteenth-century head ornament (Lalaat) along with forehead and head ornaments (sheersh alankar) in three pieces are made in gold and studded with rubies and pearls. This set is from South India. (National Museum, New Delhi.)

the inlaying and overlaying of iron in steel articles and it has a long history in Asia and Egypt, as well as Europe. The Mughal period's manifestation of such decorations continues a tradition, which had its beginnings in Iran during the medieval period. '

According to Rustam J. Mehta, 'Now, with passing of time the need for damascene weapons of war has completely disappeared and the skill of the craftsmen is devoted to ornamenting boxes, *surahis* (large vessels to hold water), flower vases, salvers, knives, scissors, betel-nut cutters, hookah bases and such other articles of daily use. Muslim craftsmen show an admirable skill and pride in the laying of wire to form verses from the Quran, verses of poetry and prayers to bring good fortune.

Probably skilled artisans produced damascened swords, daggers, elephant goads and even shields to a very limited extent and mostly for ceremonial purposes.'

In Sirohi, a background of frosted silver was arranged around the gold pattern. This became the characteristic feature of damascening from Sirohi, although this style was also followed by other states, (such as Sialkot) it became more or less particular and confined to Sirohi.

Arms produced in Jaipur were engraved on damascened steel. Another important centre of damascened arms was Hyderabad, where the work was done in silver and gold.

In the twentieth century large quantities of damascened works were produced in Gujarat, Sialkot, Jaipur, Alwar, Sirohi and Lahore. The items were mainly steel plates engraved with a minute arabesque design, into which silver and gold wires were hammered. This kind of inlay work is known as *teh nashan* or deep *koftgari* of which

there are various forms or qualities. In this type of work, the steel is deeply engraved and thick gold or silver wire is hammered into the grooves. It is then filed down, cleaned and blued, by repeated firings until the surface is completely smooth and polished. Sometimes both gold and silver are used and the style is known as Ganga-Jamuna. This is like *koftgari* but gold and silver wires are used in the same design, and the gold is often alloyed with a little copper to give it a pinkish tinge. The surface is then rendered blue through firing. This pattern is named after the rivers Ganga and Yamuna, which meet at Allahabad and flow together to the sea but maintain the distinct colour of their water for some distance. The water of the Ganga is described in literature as white while that of the Yamuna is deep blue. Therefore, when the same patterns of two colours run side by side, the object is said to be of the Ganga-Yamuna·patterns. In the case of ordinary or shallow *koftgari*, the design is engraved in shallow grooves or scratchings into which a very fine wire is hammered. The amount of silver and gold employed is accordingly very small. Consequently, the surface cannot be polished and smoothened as in the *teh nashan* or deep *koftgari* without removing or damaging the inlaid gold and silver wire. Whereas the inlaid wire cannot

Damascened jewellery boxes now in the collection of the National Museum, New Delhi.

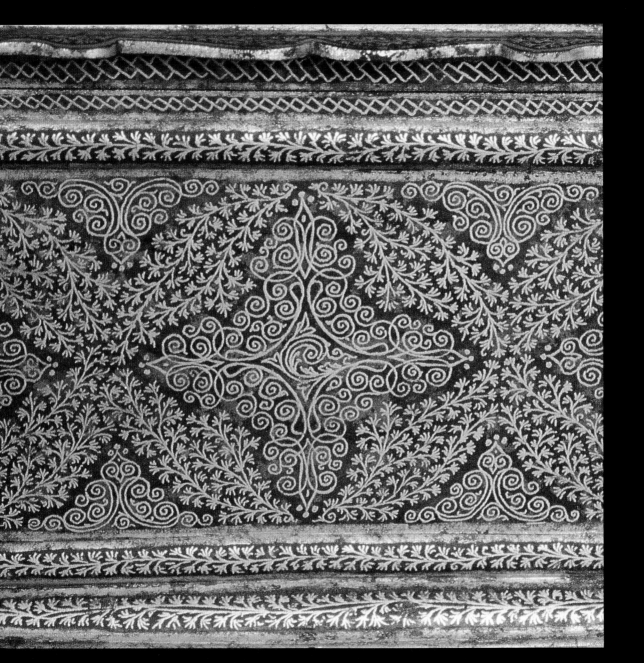

*These details from a damascened box **(facing page)** and a bidri plate **(above),** show the perfection of the craftsman's art. (National Museum, New Delhi.)*

be felt in *koftgari* of a good quality, in the cheaper forms of *koftgari*, the wire can be readily felt on the surface.

The cheapest form of this technique is a sort of imitation *koftgari* known as *dewali*. In this case, the surface is smoothened with a file after which a pumice stone is used. The pattern is scratched with a stylus and lime juice sprinkled over it to thoroughly clean the surface. The surface is then heated and the gold leaf to be applied is lifted with a pair of pincers and lightly hammered, and rubbed down with a *mori* stone. This causes the gold to adhere to the portions of the surface containing the pattern that has been starched out to receive it.

In Rajasthan a fourth system prevailed where portions of the gold leaf were scratched out to remove it from the base metal producing a closer similarity to wire inlaying

Kerala (the old Travancore part) may be said to have a style of *koftgari* of its own, which consists of items made of rough steel with gold wire beaten into it in the form of a floral design.

BIDRI

~

Damascening in silver is called bidri, and derives its name from Bidar, earlier part of the Nizam's territory, now in Andhra Pradesh. This is the highest

form of art practised in India after enamelling and the craft is still practised in Bidar.

Bidar is located about seventy-five miles from Hyderabad in the Deccan and in ancient times was the seat of the Hindu kingdom of the same name. After its conquest by Muslim invaders, it continued to be the seat of the Bahmani Dynasty of Muslim rulers.

It is commonly believed that one of the Hindu kings of Bidar invented the craft of bidri ware, using the articles thus decorated to hold flowers and other offerings in honour of his household gods. In any case, it cannot, be disputed that the quality of bidri ware improved and reached its zenith under the patronage of the Muslim sovereigns who fostered the crafts and encouraged and supported the local artisans. Referring to bidri ware, Professor Speight observed: 'Bidri ware is indeed a product of craftsmanship worthy to rank alongside the carved wooden work of Mysore and Kashmir, the metal work of Madras and Benares, the carved ivory of Travancore and the lamps and sacrificial vessels of Nepal.'

According to Rustam J. Mehta, 'Two kinds of bidri work used to be produced in Purniah during the closing of the nineteenth century. The better type was the *gharki* in which the

designs were deeply cut and the articles were very well finished. The other, *karna-bidri* showed much simpler patterns and the vessels were rather inferior in finish.'

As the fame of bidri ware travelled abroad, a host of modern articles are produced today for sale to tourists. They consist of boxes of all kinds, book ends, tea pots, cigarette cases, ashtrays, tourist dishes and so on. Bidri work is particularly used to make hookah bases, *pandans,* and in

A splendid plate worked in bidri. *(National Museum, New Delhi.)*

Enamelling as an art form has yielded several masterpieces. Seen here is a sword hilt and fittings set. (National Museum, New Delhi.)

ware is also made in Benares but the alloy used in Benaras consists of zinc and copper. In Lucknow the main metal is zinc, the others being lead, tin and copper, each added in the proportion of one by sixteenth of the quantity of zinc. Although in Hyderabad, zinc was gradually reduced and the quantity of lead was increased, in Murshidabad lead is completely omitted.

The desired vessel is first moulded, and then reduced to the exact shape on a turning lathe. It is then engraved or chased in various depths according to the quality or kind of bidri to be produced. After smoothening and polishing the object, it is coloured with a dark black or green colour by means of a paste of sal ammoniac and saltpetre moistened with rapeseed oil and thickened with charcoal. In Murshidabad and Lucknow blue vitriol is added. The vessel is slightly heated by placing it in the sun, and then rubbed with a little oil. The colour thereby tends to become permanent. Bidri does not rust but it breaks if handled with extreme roughness.

There are two main forms of bidri as in *koftgari*, according to the depth of embedding and quality of the metal fixed to the surface. These are known

articles where the use of more precious metals is not feasible. Apart from being one of the highest art forms, bidri work has some unique qualities —it never fades and if tarnished the shine can be easily restored. This work is done on a black coloured base metal and it is always inlaid with silver. To make bidri ware, an alloy of tin and copper in proportion of twenty-four parts of tin to one part of copper is used as the base metal. This kind of as *teh nashan* or deeply cut work and *zar nashan* or *zar buland* or raised work. According to the explanation given by T.N. Mukherji when explaining the process of *zar buland,* 'Thin plates of gold or silver (are) laid on a bed of wax and resin, which prevents their moving about and serves as a glue when pressed on the ground work. A small piece of paper is next inserted into the cavities made on the surface of the vessel, to take an impression of the excavated pattern. It is taken out and placed on the gold or silver leaf, which is cut into the exact measure thus obtained. The piece is then taken up by the top of the fingers and the chisel, placed on its corresponding cavity, into which it is firmly inserted by a steel point, and gently hammered in.' And he continues: 'very thin leaf is used for the ordinary kinds, while in the more durable workmanship, gold or silver wire is employed.'

In *teh nashan* the pattern is deeply etched and silver or gold wire, which is cut to the exact shape and size of the chased pattern embedded on to the pattern. After the wire is embedded on to the pattern on the object, the surface is smoothened and polished, the silver and gold ornamentation of the object lies within or below the surface.

Zar nashan or *zar buland* work resembles Tanjore encrusted ware to a large degree. Once the outline of the pattern is engraved, a silver leaf is held over the pattern and rubbed with a finger until a tracing of the design is imparted on the surface of the leaf. The leaf is then cut into the desired pieces according to the pattern with each piece being a little larger than the space to be covered. The margin or rim of each silver leaf is bent over, and the resulting cavity thus formed is filled with a piece of soft lead. Then it is pressed into the engraved outline and hammered all over the metal surface to keep the applied piece in position. In the final process the silver leaf is chased on the surface on the completion of the pattern.

A form of *zar nashan* exists in Sialkot, in which the base metal is brass and the finished article is overlaid with both silver and gold. But the process followed here is different from that of any of the centres of

bidri. In this style the pattern is partially engraved; the silver and gold is fixed within the grooves, and then worked up on to the surface by chasing and punching the pattern. This gives a richer effect of ornamentation than what is produced by other simple forms of encrusted decoration.

In Bidar, the floral decoration is generally drawn in a manner that is more or less in keeping with nature. The oldest pattern is that of a poppy flower, a design that occurs all over India. During the Mughal period the *kimkhab* weavers belonged to the various regions of India. They wove fabric, which consisted of one thread of silk and one thread of zari, which was used as the warp *(tana)* and the weft *(bana)*. The silk thread of the textile was on the back while the zari thread was displayed on the front. The pattern was produced by zari. It gave a rich and shiny effect, while the inner side of the fabric was smooth. The whole weaving gave a brocade-like effect. These days this textile is made in Benaras as well. The weavers frequently produce this poppy motif in which the leaves are shown in silver and flowers in gold. After the poppy flower, the most popular design—in which wire alone makes for minute and intricate ornamentation—has silver crosses or stars placed in an assorted or in a diagonal fashion.

In Murshidabad and Purnea wire alone is never used, but silver and gold leaves in fairly large patches are cut in the form of flowers and animals, which are then deeply embedded and polished along with the surface. Polishing is a characteristic of the bidri of Bengal and Bihar. In Purnea, the flower decoration is always conventional. Sometimes the designs that can be seen on bidri ware are Chinese or oriental in character, the influence of the art of Sikkim and Bhutan is evident in this case.

A few hookah bowls in gold and flower vases in silver bidri have been produced in Kashmir. The designs in these are worked in wire embedded below the surface, but remarkably, very little wire is used, much less than in any other form of bidri ware. The design may be said to be invariably covering the whole surface in a scroll design.

The art of manufacturing bidri in Lucknow must have been carried over from Bidar during the period of the Awadh Nawabs. Earlier the work was very different from Bidar and similar to *zar buland*. In this style, large patches of silver leaf in the form of fish, flowers and leaves are encrusted all over the surface. In due time, this changed to a style in which realistic designs were produced in a minute and complex manner much after the fashion had evolved in Purnea and Murshidabad.

In Murshidabad and Purnea wire alone is never used, but silver and gold leaf in fairly large patches is cut in the form of flowers and animals, which are then deeply embedded and polished along with the surface. Polishing is a characteristic of the bidri of Bengal and Bihar.

OTHER METALWARE

Facing page and **above**: *Richly worked water vessels in encrusted ware.*
(National Museum, New Delhi.)

With beautiful floral designs, this example of painted lacware is from Moradabad. (National Museum, New Delhi.)

~

There are some other techniques which—though distinctively apart—resemble enamelware. Lac-coloured metal ware, tinned-ware, encrusted ware and niello ware fall in this category.

LAC-COLOURED METALWARE

This is an old art of great importance in many centres, the most reputed of which are Moradabad, Jaipur, Kashmir and Peshawar. The main centre of lac-coloured metal ware is Moradabad in Uttar Pradesh. In this technique, the design is chased on the metal surface and the engravings thus made are filled with black lac or of lac in various colours, applied with a hot bolt. The hot bolt used in this technique fuses or distributes the lac over the surface of the object. The excess lac that overflows the boundaries of the design is removed by cleaning the surface with sand or brick dust and water or with sand paper or a file. The surface is then polished and the pattern shows through with the colours embedded within the metallic surface.

Sometimes the objects are gilded or tinned and the coloured ornamentations shown up on a gold, silver or a tinned background. Once the copper vessels are tinned, an extensive background is punched or chased on the surface of the object. This results in the floral decorations showing up in relief while the depressions are filled with the black-coloured lac and fused. The whole then resembles a floral design on a white metal background. Interestingly, this form is known locally as bidri. Earlier the patterns were bold, but successive

A copper samovar from Kashmir. (National Museum, New Delhi.)

developments engendered a more refined style known as *marori* and later on, a form called *charakwan* evolved. In the latter, the pattern is in black or other different coloured lac while the background is brass. In some examples, the surface is engraved between the scrolls and filled in with a black-coloured lac.

By the end of the nineteenth century, some examples in *marori* and *charakwan* work were produced in Jaipur. An outstanding example is a beautiful shield with a scene from the *Ramayana* on a field of lac with red roses and green leaves. In later years, other mythological scenes came to be engraved and ornamentally covered with coloured lac on a metallic surface.

Lac had been used in Kashmir for a long time for the purpose of colouring brass and copper vessels but during the beginning of the twentieth century the use of lac for this purpose came to an end.

In Moradabad, the depressions of the designs are filled with black or coloured lac. A unique example of coloured lac painted-ware from Moradabad is a modern brass vase decorated with red flowers and green leaves on a white background in a diamond-shaped frame which is painted with coloured lac. Around the second quarter of the twentieth century, the process of producing elaborate designs on a coloured background was discontinued and was substituted by coloured designs on a metallic surface in Moradabad and Jaipur as well, since it could be done faster and was cheaper too. However, the bright colours started to fade in a few weeks which led to the early demise of this craft.

TINNED WARE

~

Tinned metal ware was mainly found in Kashmir and northern Punjab. This craft had its origin in Persia where these vessels were used for the purpose of cooking. The origin of ornamentation on tinned ware is therefore obviously Islamic in nature.

There are various styles and patterns that are still in use, of which, there are several designs in Kashmir. Among these is the floral rosette on a black background that consists of an assortment of numerous small flowers on a spirally twisted line, which passes all around the object. Other designs sport elongated, flamboyant figures that, on first sight, convey the impression of being composed of Arabic inscriptions arranged geometrically.

J.L. Kipling, then curator of the Lahore Central Museum, described this Kashmir craft in 1878. According to him, 'Articles to be engraved are first shaped from a sheet of copper or brass, seldom cast, excepting the handles; knobs, hinges etc.

'The pattern is traced with a steel stylus and is then cut with great rapidity with a hammer and small chisels or punches. When the engraving is complete the object is heated and the ground is filled in with heated lac; after which it is rubbed with deodar charcoal, which polishes the plain surface and removes the superfluous lac. The work is again heated and rubbed till the lac has lost its shine, and a dead black deposit is left in the incised parts. The whole is then tinned in the usual way, the lac acting as a reserve and stopping out the tin.'

According to Kipling, this type of work was also done at Peshawar and at Amritsar, but it was never of the same superior quality as that of Kashmir. As for the latter 'compared with older samples, it will be seen that

A tinned ware tray, with fine tracing. (National Museum, New Delhi.)

~

the modern work is neater, smaller, and less bold in character.'

Earlier, Kashmir used to manufacture copper, not tinned ware, with arabesque design showing on a gold and sometimes even on a gilt surface. The style of ornamentation differs from that of Kashmir in Peshawar and northern Punjab, as here the copper was chased and not loaded with lac or other pigment. It was usually a preparation of lamp-black and not of coloured lac. In Kashmir, tin is soldered on copper, which has been earlier engraved deeply with a diffused floral design. These depressions were then filled with a black composition, which resembled niello work. The objects were studded all over with slightly raised flowers on a background of blackened foliated scrolls, so that the stars shone like frosted silver.

Sometimes tinned copper vessels are simply chased, with a red or copper pattern showing through the white metal surface. In Moradabad, tin is soldered on brass and incised through to the brass in floral patterns, which are simply marked sometimes by the

An example of encrusted
work, this tray depicts
Radha and Krishna
in a romantic grove.
(National Museum,
New Delhi.)

yellow outlines of the brass. The Moradabad craftsmen also engraved the pattern either in *sada* (plain) or *sia kalam*. In the former style, a floral design is generally incised or engraved on the brass article, which has been previously tinned so that the 'gold' and

further embellished with frosted decorations or small perforations, (the engraving may or may not be filled with coloured lac).

In the *sia kalam* style, the actual ornamentation is embossed in low relief or the engraving is done to bring

the brass shine through the incised lines of the design against the tinned background.

Sometimes the process is carried a little further and the areas inside the engraved lines of the pattern are

the floral design into low relief, sometimes against a minutely chased background. The depressions are filled with coloured lac, leaving the floral scroll of the design in the golden yellow of the brass. Today, interior work, white, red and green synthetic lacquers are used instead of the lac.

'The oldest and the best of Moradabad work is marked by bold and simple outlines, not overloaded with details; the modern tendency is to decrease the artistic effect by minute enrichment and too complicated tracery.' No wonder 'the elegant shape of the vessels with their rich floriated patterns standing out in their gold or silvery brightness on a black ground soon attracted the attention of the foreign visitors, and their sale went up by leaps and bounds.'

ENCRUSTED WARE

Encrusted work is an art used for the ornamentation of one metal surface through the application on to it of one or more metals. Encrusted ware comes in two types—one with the applied metal raised above the surface and the other, below the surface.

Two kinds of encrusted ware exist in South India. The first is *swami* work of Thanjavur, Tamilnadu. In Thanjavur, the applied portions stand out in bold relief. This can be seen as large trays of copper covered with silver encrustation in *swami* form,

copper bowls in original *swami* design and circular brass plates with silver *swami* work produced in Tanjore. *Swami* work is peculiar to South India, and represents in *alto-relievo* or embossed style, distinct designs or figures of deities or *swamis* of the Hindu pantheon. As local craftsmen render this work, it cannot be found in many regions in its original form although the depiction of gods and goddess on jewellery is common to all regions of India. The deities, all identified by inscriptions giving their south Indian names, include Vishnu (and his fish, or *Matsya*, incarnation), Shiva, Ganesha and Sarasvati. Some specimens are covered all over with encrustations of a leaf pattern of silver on copper and in one case, silver encrusted on brown waxy copper.

The second type of encrusted ware is from Tirupati, in Andhra Pradesh, where the applied metal is smooth and level with the surface. Brass trays, bowls, dishes and decorative pieces with copper and silver encrustation were made here. These items were, however, more for the purpose of decoration and not for everyday use. They were used on special occasions and were mainly used as decorative items. Originally only two metals—brass and copper—were used in this

work. However, the use of silver was introduced later, which pointed to a European influence. Unfortunately, the pressures of mass production have led now to the substitution of large patches of fine silver leaf, stamped with a die. This replaces the multitude of small hand-crafted pieces of silver leaf, which were earlier used for the purpose of ornamentation. In Tiruchirapalli (Tamil Nadu), a very curious process of encrustation exists where brass vessels are encrusted on the surface with zinc.

PAINTED WARE

~

Painted metal wares are produced in Belgaum, Bareilly and Tilhar. The colours used are mostly aspilnal—red and gold—and the designs implemented are mythological, ancient and distinctly oriental in nature.

TURQUOISE WARE

~

Produced in Kashmir, this work started towards the end of the nine-teenth century and is totally different from bidri work. It is a sort of mosaic

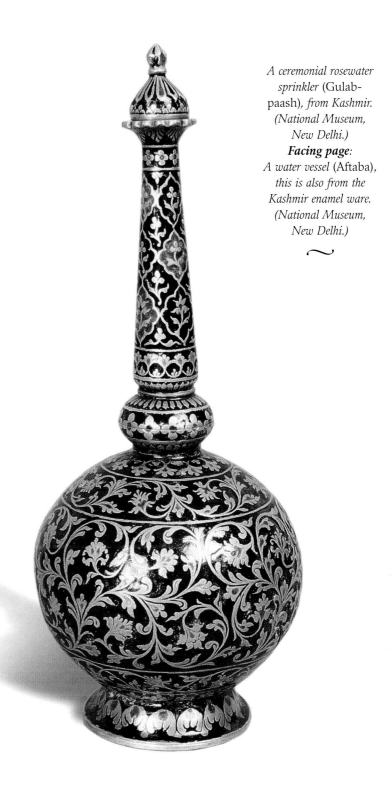

A ceremonial rosewater sprinkler (Gulab-paash), *from Kashmir. (National Museum, New Delhi.)*
Facing page: *A water vessel* (Aftaba), *this is also from the Kashmir enamel ware. (National Museum, New Delhi.)*
~

in brass, in which the recesses of the pattern are compacted with fragments of turquoise embedded in cement.

NIELLO WARE

Niello may be regarded as a form of enamelling, but this old art still survives only in one or two localities of Burma. Decoration of swords and other arms was done in niello work. The designs generally are floral or scroll engraved deeply in the basic metal and the lines of the pattern are filled in with an alloy of copper, silver and lead to produce a black effect. This is now an art forgotten by the craftsmen of India, although it appears possible that, earlier on, knowledge of this art did exist possibly in Kashmir. Only one example, a small perfume bottle from Kashmir, was on display in the exhibition in 1903 entitled 'Indian Art at Delhi'. The pattern executed on it was quite different from the designs of the area of its declared origin, but the owner claimed that it had been made in Kashmir.

The technique to make niello ware requires the purest silver on which the design is first punched and then chased in order to lower the background of the design. The hollows thus created are filled with a mixture consisting of two parts lead, one part silver and one part copper. The object is then positioned in a charcoal furnace, in which fragments of coconut shell are placed to give off a thick black smoke. This helps in

accentuating the black tinge that the object is to acquire. The object is left in the furnace until all the materials fuse and unite with the silver.

The flux used in this work is a mixture of crude sulphate of ammonia and sulphur. The excess colouring material is rubbed off and the silver is then polished. The design in bright, shining silver appears on a black field.

It is thus similar to enamelling, which is very effective and permanent. This art is not popular due to two reasons— the very demanding nature of its process and because it requires a very high temperature for the fusion of the metals, it is a health hazard also, as the sulphurous fumes that are produced by the furnace can impair the craftsman's well-being.

SELECT READING LIST

Bala Krishnan, R. Usha	*Dance of the Peacock: Jewellery Traditions of India,* India Book House, 2001, Government of India Publication.
Bala Krishnan, R., Usha	*Jewels of the Nizams,* India Book House, 2001, Government of India Publication.
Birdwood, George	*The Industrial Arts of India*, Reprinted, London, 1971.
Brij Bhushan, Jamila	*Indian Metalware,* First edition, 1961.
Brij Bhushan, Jamila	*Indian Jewellery and Ornaments and Decorative Designs*, Taraporewala Sons & Co. Ltd. Bombay, 1955.
Chandra, Rai Govind	*Indo-Greek Jewellery*, New Delhi, 1979.
Fazl, Abu'l	*Ain-i-Akbari,* Translated by H. Blockmann, 3rd edition, New Delhi, 1977.
Hendley, T.H.	*Indian Jewellery, Journal of Indian Art and Industry*, Vol. XII, Nos. 95-07.
Hendley, T.H.	*Indian Jewellery*, London, 1909.
Jacob, S.S. and Hendley, T.H.	*Jeypore Enamels*, London, 1886.
Jain, J.	*India Magazine,* Vol. VII, *The Skill of the Hands,* 1986.
Keen, Manuel and Kaouki, Salam	*Treasury of the World, Jewelled Arts of India in the Age of the Mughals*, Thames & Hudson, 2001.
Krishnadasa, Rai	*'The Pink Enamelling of Benaras' Chhavi, Golden Jubilee volume,* Vol. I. Bharat Kala Bhavan, Benares, 1971.
Kumar, Meera Sushil	*Traditions of India*, India Books House Ltd., Bombay, 2001.

Marshall, John	*Taxila*, 3 Vols., Cambridge, 1951.
Mehta, J. Rustam	*The Handicrafts and Industrial Arts of India,* First edition, Taraporevala Sons & Co. Ltd., Bombay, 1960.
Morley, G.	*'On Applied Art of India in Bharat Kala Bhavan'. Chhavi, Golden Jubilee Volume,* Benares, 1971.
Maryon	*Metal works and enamelling.*
Nigam, M.L.	*Jewellery-Inlaywork and studding of Gems,' History of Technology in India*, Vol. I, Indian National Science Academy, New Delhi, 1997.
Nigam, M.L.	*Indian Jewellery*, Roli Books Pvt. Ltd. 1999.
Skelton, Robert (ed.)	*'Arts of the Goldsmith', The Indian Heritage, Court Life and Arts Under Mughal Rule*, Victoria & Albert Museum, London, 1982.
Stronge, Susan; Smith, Nima and Harle, J.C.	*A Gold Treasury, Jewellery from the Indian Sub-continent,* Victoria & Albert Museum, Indian Art Series, Reprinted 1995, London.
Untracht, O.	*Traditional Indian Jewellery of India*, Thames and Hudson, London, 1997.
Watt, George	*Indian Arts at Delhi*, Calcutta, 1903.

PHOTO CREDITS